10/20/97

To Mike Burg

THE BATTLE OF GRISWOLDVILLE

FIELDS OF GRAY

Gary Livingston

CAISSON PRESS
Cooperstown, New York

CONTENTS

LIST OF MAPS

PREFACE

Why, I've been asked, did you write a book on The Battle of Griswoldville? There were several reasons. First, very little has been written about the battle. Secondly, most major works on the Civil War only mention it in a paragraph or two and then only to criticize the battle for ever being fought. Modern historians have called the battle an, "exercise in futility". Past historians have been quoted as saying it was, "unnecessary, unexpected, and utterly unproductive of any good...(it) will be remembered as an unfortunate accident whose occurrence might have been avoided by the exercise of proper caution and circumspection." Another book would say of Sherman's March, "There was plenty of food, no fighting, and marches that could be made in a few hours." There was a fight. The battle did happen, men did die for a cause they believed in on a cold November day in Griswoldville, Georgia.

The Georgia troops made up entirely of militia and other state units, were faulted for frontally attacking the entrenched veteran Northern troops. "Why would they do that?", people would ask me. These weren't grizzled Confederate veteran soldiers. They were citizen soldiers of the South.

This battle and this war was fought in a time when honor meant more to most men than death. These Georgia boys and men had been ridiculed for years for not belonging to the regular Southern army. They wanted to prove their manhood, to do the honorable thing.

No one questions the troops who advanced in "Picketts Charge", or the soldiers who charged frontally at Fredericksburg with the Union Irish Brigade, or the Confederates who followed General Cleburne forward at Franklin. They were veteran troops fighting far from home. The Georgia troops at Griswoldville had more of a reason to advance up that hill than the men in those veteran commands. The Georgians had just past through a burned out Griswoldville that had been put to the torch by Union troops. These citizen soldiers were the only troops between Sherman's army and their homes and loved ones in this part of Georgia. They fought a gallant fight on a cold November day in 1864. Nothing more could be asked of these young boys, men and old men from Georgia.

I wrote, *Fields of Gray, The Battle of Griswoldville*, to fill this gap in our understanding of this battle and why it was fought and why the Georgia troops stood alone against Sherman's army. To try and answer the many questions of this battle, I have traced the campaign in its entirety, from its beginnings in Sherman's burning of Atlanta, his move eastward, the Battle of Griswoldville and the bitter Southern retreat back to Macon. I have tried to address each of these elements of the campaign in detail, chronologically.

ACKNOWLEDGMENTS

I would like to thank my Mother for creating an interest in books and writing as a young boy in Macon, Georgia. To my late Father who, when I was a young boy, took me to the battlefields of Lookout Mountain and Chickamauga which created my interest in the Civil War. My family moved to Georgia in the Mid-40's from the coalfields of western Pennsylvania. At age five, I remember a saleswoman coming to our home in Macon, Georgia and selling my Mother a set of encyclopedias'. The saleswoman was showing us the books and when she turned to the section on the Civil War and Sherman's march to the sea, she began to cry. The "March" was still very vivid in the minds of most of the Georgia people. I would like to thank my two older brothers, Harry Jr. and Frank who played Rebels to my being a Yankee. After we moved back to the northeast, I switched sides and became a Rebel with my younger brother Mark playing the side of the Yankee. I suppose, even now, I still hear the guns.

Thanks to the Augusta, Athens, Atlanta and Macon Libraries for their assistance in providing research materials. Also, to Mr. Carl Anderson who scrapped the bottom of the research barrel to come up with much needed information on the Battle of Griswoldville.

I presently reside in James Fenimore Cooper's hometown of Cooperstown, New York. I would like to thank our local town library, the Cooperstown Village Library for their assistance. The New York State Historical Association Research Library, also of Cooperstown. I owe thanks to Tom Malone and the Cooperstown Civil War Round Table who, like thousands of other groups of its kind across the nation, keep the memory of the men who fought in this great conflict alive.

Two excellent books, and a magazine article, which included

accounts of the battle, were my signposts in writing this manuscript. Jim Miles, *To the Sea*, William Scaife's, *The March to the Sea* with his excellent map of the of the Battle of Griswoldville which helped me immensely and William Harris Bragg's article in Civil War Times Magazine, *A Little Battle of Griswoldville.*

I've always wondered why all writers thank their wives for all the help and assistance in the writing of their books. After writing this book I understand. Thanks to my wife, Terry, for all of her help, patience and most of all understanding. Same for my daughter's, Shay, Paige and Kim.

1   Hurricane Sherman

Thirteen year old Bridges Smith was working in the Macon arms factory in central Georgia when word spread fast throughout the city and the factory that the dreaded day had arrived. Sherman's army would soon be on the march, and most likely central Georgia would be his intended target. Bridges Smith knew what he had to do for he had rehearsed it in his mind every day since General Hood's Army of Tennessee had retreated from Atlanta, then from Georgia, leaving it almost defenseless. Smith although a factory worker, was also a private in the Georgia Militia. Upon hearing the call to arms, he left to join his comrades of the 5th Regiment, Georgia Militia. Bridges Smith and the other Georgia troops of the 5th Regiment were soon on their way to Camp Lovejoy located at Lovejoy Station, Georgia. At Camp Lovejoy they were soon joined by the rest of the Georgia state troops in protecting the most direct route into Macon.[1]

The order to assemble the State forces had been received by their commander, Maj. Gen. Gustavus W. Smith on October 12, 1864. The total Georgia force that gathered at Camp Lovejoy would be a little more than 2,800 infantrymen, 200-300 local reserve cavalry and three batteries of attached artillery. Brigadier-General Alfred Iverson with two brigades of cavalry covered his front[2]

These troops were mostly composed of a hodgepodge of factory workers, city guards, railroad patrols, State and county officers, some having been honorably discharged on account of wounds or failing health and a number of men who had for one reason or another been exempted from Confederate military service. These men were known as Governor Joseph Brown's "pets" throughout the south. The troops gathered at Camp Lovejoy had all been called back from a thirty day "harvest" furlough, granted earlier by Joe Brown. The Confederate regulars also called these state units "cradle and grave" units, for they were usually made up of boys younger than sixteen and men older than sixty years of age.₃

A typical company in the Georgia Militia would be composed of men usually from the same county or city, not unlike the regular Confederate army companies. They were relatives, neighbors and friends who grew up together in the same areas of Georgia. They were similar in make up to the troops of Company C, 7th Regiment, commanded by Col. Abner F. Redding. This company belonged to Anderson's Brigade, Georgia Militia. The Company commander was Capt. John J. McArthur. The entire company hailed from Montgomery County, located between Macon and Savannah, and had been enrolled in April, 1864. The roster originally had 30 men listed but by October, 1864, due to the fighting around Atlanta, was down now to approximately 27 members. The roster of Co. C:

> 1st Lt. Gipp Wilcox
> 2nd Lt. Walter T. McArthur
> 3rd Lt. J. W. Vaughn
> 1st Sgt. M. C. Adams

Pvt. G. W. Adams	Pvt. Elkana Haralson
Pvt. John Adams	Pvt. _____ Haralson
Pvt. M. B. Adams	Pvt. John W. McArthur
Pvt. Thomas B. Adams	Pvt. Addison McArthur
Pvt. Groves Connor	Pvt. Allen McArthur
Pvt. Joe K. Conner	Pvt. David Morrison
Pvt. James J. Conner	Pvt. Daniel Q. Morrison
Pvt. Martin Cauey	Pvt. Duncan D. McRae
Pvt. Littleton Clark	Pvt. William Ryals
Pvt. Orien Clark	Pvt. Uriah Sears
Pvt. Andrew J. Gillis	Pvt. C. R. Vaughn ₄

Looking at the roster, it listed five soldiers with the last name of Adams, three with Conners, five McArthurs and two Clarks, Vaughns, Morrisons and Harralsons. Fathers, sons, brothers, cousins, uncles, all serving together in the same company and enlisted from the same area. Company C from Montgomery County was a typical unit in the Georgia Militia.₅

General Gustavus W. Smith's 1st Division Georgia Militia was composed of the 1st Brigade (Carswell's) now commanded now by Col. James N. Willis. The 2nd Brigade was commanded by Brig. Gen. Pleasant J. Phillips. Second in command of the 2nd Brigade was Col. James Mann. The 3rd Brigade was under the command of Brig. Gen. Charles D. Anderson and the 4th Brigade was commanded by Brig. Gen. Henry K. McCay.₆

The Georgia State Line was a unique and relatively elite state unit, composed of 400 men of conscription age veterans, consisting of the 1st & 2nd Regiments. They would also join General Smith's militia at Camp Lovejoy. They were commanded by Georgia Lt. Col. Beverly D. Evans. Colonel Evans' brother, Brigadier General N. G. Evans, served elsewhere in the Confederate army.₇

The attached artillery was commanded by Capt. Ruel W. Anderson and consisted of 4-12 pounders "Napoleons". Captain Anderson had been appointed October 15, 1863 to Company B in the Pulaski Artillery attached to the Fourteenth Battalion, Army of Tennessee.₈

Also attached to Smith's militia and sent on to Camp Lovejoy at Lovejoy Station by their overall Georgia commander, Gen. Howell Cobb, were some home guard and work shop units from Athens and Augusta, Georgia. Again, like the State Line soldiers, they were of mostly conscription age, but were exempt from service in the regular army because of their employment in the armory or other related fields. Maj. Ferdinand W. C. Cook commanded the Athens Local Defense Battalion (23rd Infantry Battalion Georgia State Guard) and Maj. George T. Jackson commanded the Augusta Local Defense Battalion also known as the Augusta Arsenal Battalion.₉

The Athens Local Defense Battalion, had been formed from employees of the local armory, into a local defense unit known as the 23rd Battalion, Georgia Volunteers, separate from the rest of the home guard in Athens. The Athens press usually agreed that the armory men were superior troops, where as, in other parts of the state, the press made light of their local militia units. When the workers were called into service, the armory ceased operations until the return of the battalion from duty.[10]

Major Ferdinand Cook was commissioned as major-commandant and his brother was made captain in the Athens Battalion. Major Cook, in his dual job, ran the Athens armory and organized the defenses that were built to protect it. The battalion's jobs included not only working in the armory, but as Georgia infantrymen, they were expected to man the armories defenses in Athens. This battalion was armed with the Enfield-style rifles that they helped manufacture at the Athens armory. In addition they would be called upon to serve elsewhere in the state in emergencies, alongside the Georgia Militia. The Athens as well as the Augusta Battalion were both called into service in the summer of 1864 with General Sherman's invasion of Georgia. They had served that summer with the militia in the battle for Atlanta. Both units had served alongside Hood's regular army soldiers in that losing campaign.[11]

Saying goodbye to wives, families and again leaving their jobs and posts, the militia and the other state units, made their way along the dusty clay roads of central Georgia to the town of Lovejoy Station where they then settled in at Camp Lovejoy.

The Georgia troops were kept busy improving their defenses, trying to stay healthy and writing letters to love ones at home from their camp. Jonathan Bridges, who belonged to the ambulance unit in the Georgia Militia, was a member of Company C, 11th Regiment, 4th Brigade, under the command of Col. William T. Toole. From Lovejoy Station he would write his wife Fanny waiting at home in Stewart County, Georgia. Private Bridges hadn't heard from his wife for awhile, and like all soldiers away from home, he was hungry for news from the homefront. Private Bridges also described a sharp fight outside of Atlanta in his letter home,

Camped near Lovejoys Station
November 12, 1864

My Fanny,

I write you a few lines this morning to let you hear from me. I am well hoping you may be well and doing well. I have not received a letter from you in 10 days and am very anxious to hear from you. I have no news to write of much importance. There is a good deal of sickness in camp. E. J. HORN left for the General Hospital two days ago with a very bad spell of pneumonia. I think he is dangerous sick. BARNEY is well. I am doing very well. We have divided our mess. I am messing with three doctors and two other gentlemen and we have a Negro to cook for us. I weigh 180 lbs. I do not have much to do. I have no idea when I will get home. There is a hundred runners in camp. There was a short fight at Atlanta two days ago with the Calvary. We had three killed and 12 wounded. The Yankees had no killed. I have not heard from JOHN in some time and would like to hear from him very much. I do not know how to tell you to manage. You must manage as you think best. It seems like it is hard to get letters regular. I write every four days. I am so anxious to hear from you that if I do not get a letter regular I am like fish out of water. You can see by the way I have composed this letter that have not much to write. So I had better close it and maybe the next time I will have something that will interest you.

Your Jonathan

as ever12

Here they were, these same Georgia boys and men, four months after the Battle of Atlanta, back manning earthworks near the "Gate City". Captain Pendergrass, one of the workers in the Athens armory, moved slowly down the earthwork among his men of Company C. He passed by Privates Alex Hamuth, William Stone, John Wright and William Walker, all armed with the muskets, similar to the Enfield rifles they themselves had helped manufacture.13

Captain Adams, Company H, 5th Regiment of the 2nd Brigade, Georgia Militia, under the command of Colonel James N. Mann, filed his men in behind the old earthworks that had been erected by General Hood's army, during the summer, in the Battle of Lovejoy Station. A member of Captain Adam's company was Pvt. William Caswell who served a dual role as infantryman and litter-bearer. Also serving in the 5th Regiment, Georgia Militia, was the young Pvt. Bridges Smith, from the armament factory in Macon, who rested his rifle on the earthen bank and looked down the road toward Atlanta. Another young boy from Macon, fourteen year old Pvt. W. A. Poe, a member of Captain Butt's Home Guard, stared in the same direction waiting for something to happen. Private Poe, who had been only eleven when the war began, would be celebrating his 15th birthday on December 2, 1864, less that a month away. Pvt. Poe, along with the rest of the Georgia troops, rested in a trench and searched the horizon for a trace of blue that would herald the arrival of one of the worlds strongest armies, the dreaded veteran army of General Sherman.14

Along this defensive line were men and boys from Jones, Wilkinson, Twiggs, Monroe, Hopkins, Montgomery, Stewart, Hall, Stewart and other Georgia counties. Also at Camp Lovejoy were men from cities such as Macon, Augusta, Atlanta and Athens. Capt. Robert H. Barron, commanding a Jones County company, checked his men and then joined them in the breastworks.15

Lieutenant John Baker, Company H, 8th Regiment, commanded by Brig. Gen. Charles D. Anderson, positioned his company in the entrenchments. Also in that company were Pvts.

William Jolly and Wiley Vinson who made their way to their positions in the Southern line. All the men in Company H hailed from Jones County, located just north of Macon.

On another part of the Confederate line, two brothers both privates from Monroe County, William and James Redding were waiting and looking into the distance. Their mother Maria Searcy Redding, like a lot of mothers in Georgia, was waiting at home and worrying about her two sons. The Redding brother's father, Capt. Dan S. Redding, was also serving with the Confederacy.16

In the Georgia line was a young drummer in Company D, Pvt. Thomas S. Campbell, 4th Regiment, 2nd Brigade, Georgia Militia. The young drummer boy hailed from Hall County, Georgia. He had a brother, Warren who served as a private in Co. F, 43rd Regiment, Georgia Volunteer Infantry, Army of Tennessee.17

Further down the line Sgt. Blanton Nance was readying his Company E, 7th Regiment, Georgia Militia. The company commander was Capt. William Morgan. Pvts. William Warren and Arthur Newton along with the rest of the company hunkered down in the line and waited. Sergeant Nance, a venerable patriot of the cause, resided in Dublin, Laurens County, as did the rest of his company. Originally from Tennessee, he rendered his first military service for his country in the war of 1846-47, serving with the 1st Tennessee Cavalry, and participating in the battle of Cerro Gordo and other engagements. After the war he came south to Georgia and began farming. When the South called her soldiers to the field in 1861, though he lacked the buoyancy of youth, he manifested the same patriotic devotion and enlisted in the Brown Infantry, of Macon. It was commanded by Capt. G.A. Smith, one of the first companies to answer the first call of the governor.18

Sergeant Blanton Nance and his company were assigned to the first Georgia Battalion, and sent on to Pensacola, where hostilities seemed most imminent at the time. While on duty at Pensacola, the battle of Santa Rosa Island occurred and two artillery engagements between Fort Pickins and the Confederate batteries. From Pensacola he went to Mobile where he served the final three months of his one year enlistment. Nance was honorably discharged, and didn't see service again until the fall of 1864, when he had recently been called back to service in the militia.[19]

Georgia militiaman William Dickey thought of his wife Anna safely home and waiting for his return as he stood among members of his company. He wrote his wife regularly since being away from home.

The Georgia troops at Lovejoy Station spotted something moving toward them. There were shouts of "cavalry, cavalry". But with the dust the horses had kicked up they couldn't distinguish whether they were blue or gray troopers. As they drew nearer, they could finally make out the dusty, ragged gray uniforms of the Alabama boys from General Wheeler's cavalry. They were being driven in by the Northern cavalrymen who were hot on their heels.[20]

Two militiamen from Wilkinson County, Capt. A. A. Beall and Pvt. Henry Mercer, joined the rest of the Georgia infantrymen and watched General Wheelers cavalry ride into their lines. The Confederate cavalrymen dismounted, grabbed their weapons and joined the Georgians at the earthworks. The wait for action at Lovejoy Station, by the Georgia infantrymen, was over. If Gen. Judson Kilpatrick's calvary was at Lovejoy, General Sherman's army wouldn't be far off. [21]

2   Now you must go

General Hood's army of 36,000, including Maj. General
Wheeler's cavalry, had steadily fallen back through Georgia in
1864. Starting in late October the Army of Tennessee would
leave Lovejoy Station to go on to Palmetto, Georgia, then all the
way to Gadsden, Alabama, where General Hood would be joined
by General P. G. T. Beauregard. At Lovejoy Station Hood's
army had licked their wounds after the fighting for Atlanta.[1]

General Sherman had played General Hood's game at the
beginning of this move by leaving Maj. Gen. Henry Slocum's
Corps to occupy Atlanta and guard the crossing of the
Chattahoochee. He then preceded to move the rest of his army
the IV, XIV, XV, XVII and the XXIII Corps northward,
reaching Kennesaw on October 5th. General Sherman's army
followed the Army of Tennessee all the way to Gaylesville.
General Hood, upon hearing of Sherman's army reaching Snake
River Gap in Georgia on October 13, 1864, decided to select an
advantageous position. Hood would then turn his army about to
fight. This fight would never happen. The reason, General
Hood's officers were opposed to fighting General Sherman's
larger well trained army. In and around Gaylesville General
Sherman had grown weary of chasing an army and it's
commander that could not be made to fight. Sherman would
about face his army and return to the "gate city" of Atlanta.

It was at this time he began urging upon General Grant his
project of a march with his entire army to the sea. Before it
could be decided upon General Thomas, in Chattanooga, would
have to be made strong enough to deal with General Hood's
army on his own. General Thomas would not have to wait long.
In fact reinforcements were now on the way to join his army.[2,3]

On November 2, 1864, in correspondence to Maj.General
Thomas, General Sherman wrote: "According to Wilson's
account, you will have, in ten days, full 12,000 cavalry, and I

estimate your infantry force, independent of railroad guards full 40,000, which is a force superior to the enemy."[4]

On November 6th in a dispatch to General Grant, General Sherman gave him plans of his march through the very heart of Georgia and closes with "...I will not attempt to send couriers back, but trust to the Richmond papers to keep you well advised. I will give you notice by telegraph of the exact time of my departure."[5]

To this General Grant replies on November 7th: "I see no present reason for changing your plan; should any arise, you will see to it, or if I do, I will inform you. I think everything here favorable now. Great good fortune attend you. I believe you will be eminently successful, and at worst can only make a march less fruitful of results than hoped for." General Sherman back in Atlanta began to make plans, in his words, "To make Georgia howl." Earlier Sherman had ordered all citizens out of Atlanta. That order had been issued on September 8, 1864. In a two day exchange some 20,000-30,000 citizens were forced from Atlanta.[6]

General Sherman realized the anguished cries of protest that this policy would provoke. "If the people raise a howl against my barbarity or cruelty," He wrote to a superior, "I will answer that war is war and not popularity seeking."[7]

Mayor Calhoun of Atlanta pleaded to General Sherman on behalf of his citizens mainly consisting of women, children, the sick and elderly noting that winter was rapidly approaching. The Mayor said the act was "appalling and heartrending."[8]

General Sherman's answer was firm,

> You can not qualify war in harsher terms than
> I will. War is cruelty and cannot refine it ....You
> might as well appeal against the thunder storm as
> against these terrible hardships of war...But my
> dear sirs, when peace does come, you may call
> on me for anything. Then I will share with you
> the last cracker, and watch with you to shield
> your homes and families against danger from

every quarter.

Now you must go, and take with you your old
and feeble, feed and nurse them, and build for
them, in more quiet places, proper habitations to
shield them against the weather until the mad
passions of men cool down and allow the Union
and peace once more to settle over your old
homes at Atlanta.[9]

A Northern newspaper correspondent, who witnessed the
scenes of the evacuation of Atlanta wrote, "Old age and tottering
infants huddled together, awaiting their chance of escape. The
elderly, children and women cast many a long lingering look at
their once happy home, which they were now about to abandon,
perhaps forever."[10]

In one quick move General Sherman had rid himself of
feeding more than 20,000-30,000 hungry civilian Atlantans on a
precariously thin supply line.[11]

It was earlier in his career, during his stay at Memphis, that
General Sherman began to regard the rebellion more as a matter
of "collective responsibility", than as a simple uprising of armed
men. "It is about time the North understood the truth", he wrote
to his brother in Washington, "that the entire South, man,
woman, and child is against us...."[12]

If the South's fighting spirit was to be extinguished, General
Sherman decided, civilians as well as soldiers had to be regarded
as enemies. The war had to be made "terrible."[13]

One Illinois soldier would later write of his apprehension
about "marching out into a great unknown," where they might
"leave their bones in a strange and unfriendly land forever."[14]

The 100th Indiana, of the XV Army Corps, had been with
General Sherman's army on the chase of General Hood's army.
Beginning on October 5th, for three weeks, the 100th Indiana
Infantry and the most of the Northern army marched after the
Army of Tennessee going from Eastpoint, Georgia via Rome,
Georgia, then they crossed into Alabama near Gadsden. As
General Hood moved his army in the direction of Decatur and

Florence, General Sherman had had enough. "Damn him", General Sherman is reported as saying at the time.[15]

A private serving in the 100th Indiana Regiment, from Lima, Indiana, was Theodore F. Upson, who kept a running journal of his three years of service in the union army. Private Upson had been a part of the 350 mile chase of General Hood and was exhausted when his regiment finally returned to Atlanta, on November 8, 1864. The northern boys were cheered up when their pay was waiting for them. Private Upson would write, "Most of the boys have sent a good part of their money home."[16]

In Atlanta the 100th Indiana along with other union troops, had been kept busy ripping up railroad tracks and utterly destroying everything in the city that could be of any use to the armies of the South. Private Upson was also busy listening to rumors spreading among the Union ranks that the army would "cut loose and march south to the ocean." There were rumors of "a great campaign." Private Upson would write that, "he felt good after getting back to Atlanta" and the morale of General Sherman's army reflected that. "We would go anywhere Uncle Billy {Sherman} would lead.", he would add. [17]

Meanwhile, in Gadsden Alabama, General Beauregard and General Hood, working late into the night, agreed that General Hood should take his army into Tennessee. Both felt sure that General Sherman would surely have to leave Atlanta and follow him north. But the question arose, when should General Hood move his army forward. General Beauregard wanted the Army of Tennessee to begin as soon as possible. General Hood felt he wasn't prepared to begin his advance into Tennessee at this time and so the advance was delayed. General Sherman would later comment, "If he (Hood) will go to the Ohio River, I will give him rations, let him go north. My business is down south."[18]

On November 12, General Sherman broke his communication with the outside world. The determination to abandon Atlanta involved the undoing of much work that had been done there in the early autumn by the Union army. As the town could not be used by the Federal forces, the defenses must be destroyed, the workshops, mills, and depots must be ruined and burned. This task was turned over to a Colonel Poe, Chief Engineer of Sherman's army.[19]

David P. Conyngham, a correspondent for the *New York Herald*, who was serving in the army as a volunteer aide-de-camp with the rank of captain, stated that in Atlanta,

> Winship's iron foundry and machine shops
> were early set on fire. This valuable property
> was calculated to be worth about half a million
> of dollars. An oil refinery nearby next got on
> fire and was soon in a fierce blaze. Next
> followed a freight warehouse....The depot,
> turning tables, freight sheds, and stores around
> were soon a fiery mass.... some ruffians ran with
> brands to fire the churches...The Atlanta Hotel,
> Washington Hall and all the square around the
> railroad depot were soon in one sheet of flame.[20]

A sergeant from Michigan would write that he was about to torch a home in Atlanta when "a little girl about ten years old came to me and said, 'Mr. Soldier you would not burn our home, would you? If you do where are we going to live,' and she looked into my face with such a pleading look that I could not have the heart to fire the place so I dropped the torch and walked away." Others picked to burn Atlanta weren't so compassionate and soon Atlanta was in flames. The flames from the Gate City enabled men, sitting in the darkness, two miles distant to read letters received from faraway sweethearts. One doctor marching ten miles away swore he could read his watch by the glow.[21]

Major George Ward Nichols, an aide-de-camp to General Sherman wrote in his diary "...A grand and awful spectacle is presented to the beholder in this beautiful city now in flames...the heaven is one expanse of lurid fire."[22]

Union Colonel Oscar L. Jackson would write in his diary: "It is dark and as we look back we see that Atlanta is in flame. It will be utterly destroyed. The glare of the light against the sky is beautiful and grand. A terrible but just punishment is meted out to the gate city."[23]

A captain in the 2nd Massachusetts Volunteers, Daniel Oakey, would write,

> That nothing was to be left for the use or advantage of the enemy. The sick were sent back to Chattanooga and Nashville, along with every pound of baggage that could be dispensed with...Our communications were then abandoned by destroying the railroad and telegraph. There was something intensely exciting in this perfect isolation. At last came the familiar 'Fall In'; the great 'flying column' was on the march. [24]

The last Union troops to leave the now smoldering city, on November 15th, was the brigade of Massachusetts troops whose band played "John Brown" as they followed the armies move east from Atlanta. Captain Daniel Oakey of the Second Massachusetts volunteers would add to his journal, "Sixty thousand of us witnessed the destruction the Atlanta, while our post band and that of the Thirty-third Massachusetts played martial airs and operatic selections."[25]

General Sherman would write: "I remained in Atlanta during the 15th with the Fourteenth Corps, and the rear-guard of the right wing to complete the loading of the trains, and the destruction of the building of Atlanta which could be converted to hostile uses...".

General W. T. Sherman and his staff stayed in the city until the following morning of the 16th, then left via the Decatur road on his favorite mount, "Sam."[26]

General Sherman halted on a hill and looked back at the smoke rising to the sky. "The extremely beautiful day...The sun glancing on 55,000 gun barrels all slanted west over shoulders of men whose faces pointed east...On the Horizon white-topped wagons following the legions, 2,500 light trucks, and 600 ambulances drawn by mules and horses."[27]

A lean, strong army marched from Atlanta. They were

predominately ruddy of face and blue of eye. They were composed of yellow-haired Germans and dark-haired, blue-eyed Irish, Scotch, and English making up the bulk of the force. Men who had been burned by 3 years exposure to the hot southern sun, now swung by "Uncle Billy" on this great military gamble.[28]

Mounted on his horse General Sherman would reflect, "There was a 'devil-may-care' feeling pervading officers and men, that made me feel the full load of responsibility, for success would be expected as a matter of course, whereas, should we fail, this march would be adjudged THE WILD ADVENTURE OF A CRAZY FOOL."[29]

Among the observers on this morning were a few young Southern boys who tramped to the cities outskirts. One of the boys, Noble Williams said, "The country for miles around presented a scene of almost unequaled desolation...many trees had been fallen...the woods and fields were strewn with carcasses of dead animals...who had become disabled, were shot or left to die of starvation." The boy said the stench was sickening.[30]

A later entry in Private Upson's, 100th Indiana, diary reads... "We have utterly destroyed Atlanta."[31]

The *Macon Telegraph and Confederate Newspaper* would report that, "Atlanta has been evacuated and completely burned."[32]

Only about 50 families had remained in Atlanta, even after General Sherman's evacuation orders. In the morning some of these citizens wandered about in groups soberly inspecting the cities vast area of destruction and chaos. The hovering smoke filtered the sun's rays, giving the distressing scenes a curious amber hue.[33]

An officer in the Georgia Militia was sent by Governor Joe Brown, a week after General Sherman's army departed Atlanta, to survey the damage. Militia Gen. W. P. Howard rode to the city and reported that every factory, business, school, and 3,200 houses lay in ruin within the city. An estimated 1,800 additional houses had been put to the torch in surrounding areas. The only useful items that remained, he reported, were bricks, brass, and copper. Even the flanges of wheels on rail cars had been broken.

"In short" General Howard later wrote, "every species of machinery that was not destroyed by fire was most ingeniously broken and made worthless in its original form." General Howard also added to his report, "The crowning act of all their wickedness and villainy was committed by our ungodly foe in removing the dead from the vaults in the cemetery and robbing the coffins of the silver name plates and tippings, and depositing their own dead in the vaults."[34]

General O. O. Howard estimated that a million dollars' worth of usable material had been appropriated by Southern civilian looters after General Sherman had left the city. "There were about 250 wagons in the city on my arrival, loaded with pilfered plunder. Bushwhackers, robbers, and deserters and citizens from the surrounding country for a distance of fifty miles have been engaged in this dirty work."[35]

The thoroughness of the destruction can be realized, when we consider that by the census of 1860 Atlanta had a population of 10,000, which in 1864 had increased to 30,000. With the burning of the over 4,000 houses, including dwellings, shops, stores, mills and depots, about eleven-twelfths of the city had been destroyed.

For a few weeks, the city of Atlanta was dominated by thousands of dogs, abandoned pets who roamed in wild packs like hungry wolves. "Mans best friend had reverted to wolfish tendencies," wrote a woman who had stayed in the burned out city.[36]

An Atlanta newspaper, the *Daily Intelligencer*, would later write, "...profound silence reigned in our streets...no children in the streets, no drays, no wagons, no glorious sound of the Gospel in the churches; the theater was hushed in the silence of death. Ruin, universal ruin, was the exclamations of all."[37]

On November 15 and 16, 1864, General Sherman's army, with the smoking ruins of Atlanta to his rear, began its great march. The right wing of the army, under Maj. Gen. O. O. Howard, with General Kilpatrick's cavalry, was put in motion in the direction of Jonesborough and McDonough, Georgia with orders to make a feint on Macon and then to cross the Ocmulgee river near Planters Mills. Eventually they were to rendezvous in the neighborhood of Gordon, Georgia, in about seven days. At the same time Major-General Slocum, with the Twelfth Corps of the left wing, moved by Decatur, with orders to tear up the railroad from Social Circle to Madison and to burn the railroad bridge across the Oconee River, east of Madison. (Sherman would later claim that his army destroyed and ripped up over 100 miles of railroad track.) Slocum would then turn south, to reach Milledgeville on the same day that General Howard should reach Gordon. General Sherman would travel with the left wing to Milledgeville. Both wings had good wagon trains, loaded with ammunition and supplies, approximating 20 days' bread, 40 days sugar and coffee, with a double allowance of salt, and beef cattle sufficient for 40 days' supplies. The wagons were supplied with three days supply of grain. Each brigade commander was instructed to organize a foraging party to gather near the armies route of march such items as corn, meat and vegetables. Aiming at all times to keep in the wagon trains at least 10 days provisions. Soldiers were forbidden to enter the dwellings of the inhabitants or to commit any trespass, but were permitted, during a halt or when in camp, to gather vegetables, and to drive in stock in their front. On the march the gathering of provisions was to be left entirely to regular foraging parties.[38]

Army commanders were permitted to destroy mills, houses, cotton-gins, etc., but such destruction must only take place in regions where the army should be molested. Horses, mules, and wagons were to be appropriated as they were needed, but discrimination must be made in these captures, the rich rather than the poor being made the victims. No family was to be deprived of anything necessary to its maintenance. Able-bodied Negroes might be taken so far as this would not cause embarrassment in the matter of supplies. The troops were to start each morning at 7:00 a. m., and make about 15 miles per day. General Sherman's army of more than 70,000, including General Kilpatrick's 5,500 cavalry, 2,000 artillerymen manning 64 guns, had one destination, Savannah, Georgia and to destroy much of what lay in-between.[39]

The right wing of the Union army was led by Maj. Gen. O. O. Howard and consisted of two Corps. The XV Corp (four Divisions) was commanded by Maj.General Osterhaus. His Division Commanders were Brig. Generals Wood, Hazen, Smith and Corses. The XVII Corp (3 Divisions) was led by Maj. Gen. M. G. Blair. His Division Commanders were Maj. General Mowers and Brigadier Generals Leggetts and Smith.[40]

The Great Georgia Hurricane had begun, as the Macon *Telegraph and Confederate* newspaper would later call it,

> This Hurricane was named Sherman, and its path of destruction laid waste the heart of Georgia from Atlanta to Savannah. Loss of life and property were unbelievable. In those days, following the Hurricane, the people wrote about their losses. Those in the eye of the storm were left with nothing, while places on the edge started to return to a more normal way of life, if you can say anything was normal in November 1864.[41]

The "Sherman Hurricane" will go down in history as one of the most destructive and costly storms to hit the United States. The only buffer between "Hurricane Sherman's" 70, 000 battle hardened veterans and the heartland of the South, was Gen. Joe Wheeler's command of just under 4,000 cavalry and the just under 5,000 Georgia Militia and other assortment of Georgia units, including the Milledgeville Garrison, the Georgia Military Institute Corps of cadets, factory and penitentiary guards. This force was spread out throughout the entire central part of the state. This force was expected to provide protection for Macon, Augusta, Milledgeville and all the central portion of Georgia. A Southern force totaling just under 9,000, mostly untrained men (with the exception of Wheelers cavalry), arrayed against one of the worlds strongest and experienced armies.[42]

Union Private Jesse L. Dozer was assigned to Company A, 26th Illinois Infantry. He was 19 years of age, stood five feet, eight inches tall. He had auburn hair and blue eyes, was light complexioned and his service record listed him as a carpenter before enlisting. Private Dozier had been mustered into the service on February 27, 1864, at Springfield, Illinois. During the march he would keep a daily diary of his experiences. "On November 15th Tuesday, warm and cloudy. We marched at half past 6 in the morning...There was some skirmishing in front. We camped south east of Jonesboro the first night Dist from Atlanta 20 miles On March from south Atlanta."[43]

"November 16th 1864 Wednesday warm and cloudy....We foraged a teem of one mule & one horse & wagon We loaded it down Pork Chickens Flour & meal....We camped for the night Mcdonnel (McDonough) Georgia." Private Dozer would write in his diary.[44]

Sherman's army continued through McDonough and Jackson, Georgia. On the night of November 17, Union Colonel Oscar L. Jackson wrote in his diary, "We had only an hour and a half last night to get supper and sleep and get breakfast this morning. Have been fifty-eight hours out of Atlanta, forty-four of which we passed on the road with knapsacks. Pretty severe campaigning, but sweet potatoes are plenty and we do better."[45]

In his diary, Union Pvt. Theodore Upson, 100th Indiana, would make this entry,

> We are marching South from Atlanta. We have regularly detailed foragers under command of officers, and they find plenty of forage of all kinds. The country seems very rich. We have had but little opposition so far-now and then a few Cavalry at some cross roads or at a stream. But in a while the main body of troops marches along as though nothing had happened. Such an Army as we have I doubt if ever was got together before; all are in the finest condition. We have weeded out all the sick, feeble ones and all the faint hearted ones and all the boys are ready for meal or a fight

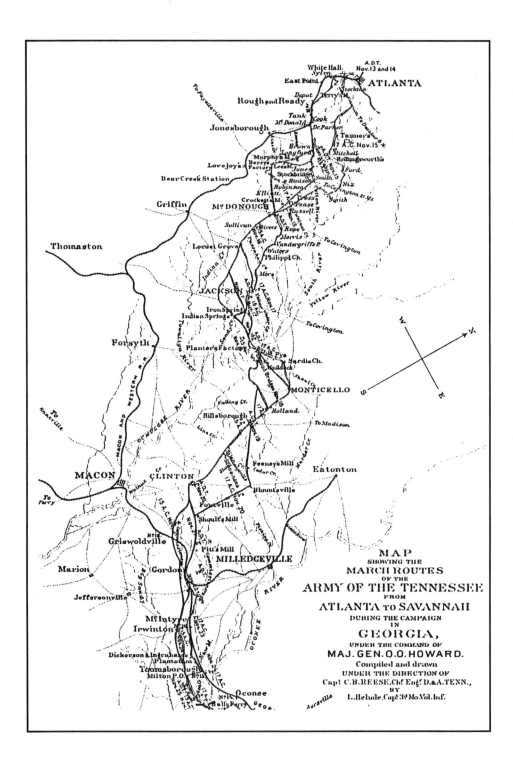

MAP
SHOWING THE
MARCH ROUTES
OF THE
ARMY OF THE TENNESSEE
FROM
ATLANTA TO SAVANNAH
DURING THE CAMPAIGN
IN
GEORGIA,
UNDER THE COMMAND OF
MAJ. GEN. O.O. HOWARD.
Compiled and drawn
UNDER THE DIRECTION OF
Capt. C.B. REESE, Chf Engr D.&A.TENN.,
BY
L. Helmle, Capt 3d Mo.Vol.Inf.

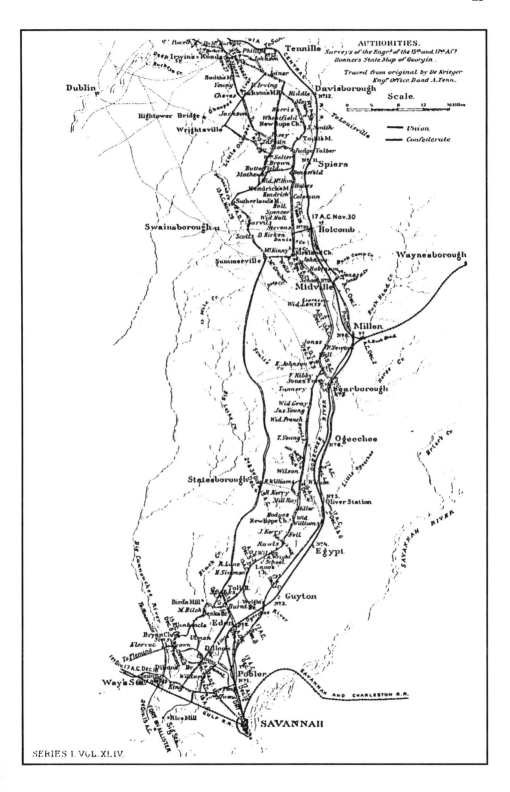

and don't seem to care which it is. We have
learned to get along with little in the way of
baggage too. All a good many carry is a blanket
made into a roll with their rubber 'poncho'
which is doubled around and tied at the ends and
hung over the left shoulder. Of course, we have
our haversacks and canteens and our guns and
cartridge boxes with 40 rounds of ammunition.
Some of the boys carry 20 more in their
pockets.[46]

Lieutenant Colonel James Austin Connolly of the 123rd
Illinois Infantry and a staff officer of the 3rd Division, XIV
Corps. would write of the burning of Atlanta, "Well the soldiers
fought for it, and the soldiers won it, now let the soldiers enjoy
it."[47]

An Orderly in the 7th Iowa Infantry would add to his journal
that he was pleased when Atlanta was burned because it "paid me
in part for the long weary days that I spent last summer behind
fortifications & dodging Rebel bullets."[48]

3   Joe Wheeler
The War Child

The Confederacy was known for producing able and flamboyant cavalry commanders and Joseph Wheeler ranks with the best of them such as J.E.B. Stuart and Nathan Bedford Forrest. Wheeler a self-professed "War Child," fought in 127 battles and skirmishes and suffered 3 wounds. He had entered the Confederate army as a lieutenant and was commissioned a major-general; at age twenty-eight he was the youngest in the Confederacy. He earned that commission after only twenty-one months of service. Sixteen horses bearing him in combat would be shot and killed out from under him.[1]

Major General Joe Wheeler stood five feet, five inches in height and weighing 120 pounds. Wheeler commanded the Army of Tennessee's cavalry in all of its major campaigns. Fighting with the Army of Tennessee he had become the country's leading expert in covering retreats. Gen. Joe Wheeler's expertise would be put to the test over the coming weeks and months.[2]

The Georgia Militia also would be put to the test in the coming days. They had been formed from what manpower that was left in the state. Mostly old men, some who had even seen action in the Mexican conflict in 1846-1847, and young boys not old enough for the regular army. The "Milish" as they were called were lampooned in the popular song "Goober Peas."

Goober Peas.
Sitting by the roadside on a summer day,
Chatting with my messmates, passing time
away
Lying in the shadow underneath the trees,

Goodness, how delicious, eating goober peas!
Chorus.
Peas! Peas! Peas! Peas! eating goober peas!
Goodness how delicious, eating goober peas!

When a horseman passes the soldiers have a rule
To cry out at their loudest: "Master, here's your
mule."
But another pleasure enchantinger than these
Is wearing out your grinders, eating goober
peas!
Chorus.
Just before the battle the general hears a row.
He says: "The Yanks are coming; I hear their
rifles now."
He turns around in wonder, and what do you
think he sees?
The Georgia militia eating goober peas.
Chorus.
I think my song has lasted almost long enough;
The subject's interesting, but the rhymes are
mighty rough.
I wish this war was over, when, free from rags
and fleas,
We'd kiss our wives and sweethearts and gobble
goober peas.

The Georgia Militia had been organized and long protected
from Confederate military service by Georgia Governor, Joseph
E. Brown. The militiamen had been widely ridiculed by the anti-
Brown press politicians, and citizens as "Joe Brown's Pets." The
regulars confederate soldiers were the ones who mostly looked
down their noses at Joe Brown's private army and felt if they
wanted to fight they should join up with them in the regular
army.[3]

The contempt for conscripts was mild in comparison to that
provoked by militia and reserves. Kate Cumming (of Georgia)

told of hearing a soldier mimicking a Georgia militiaman as "Joe Brown's Pets," were called, from the boxcar in Marietta (Georgia). "This 'Reb', he said, told piteously of his treatment, how he had been in service for two whole weeks and as yet had not received a furlough, and how he and other brave reservists were nobly defending the rear of Bragg's army." As for fighting, few full-fledged Rebs expected that of "Bob-tail militia." "They had just as well stay...(home)," wrote one of Joe Johnston's veterans in 1864, "they ain't worth a low country cow tick."4

After the war, some will explain away the fighting at Griswoldville as inexperienced soldiers led by inexperienced commanders in a needless fight. On the contrary, the commander of the Militia, Maj. Gen. Gustavus W. Smith was a graduate and former faculty member of West Point, and had served as a Confederate General. He had a reputation as being a fine engineer. He had served with the engineers in Mexico, winning two brevets. He later was a civil engineer and became New York City's street commissioner. At the Battle of Seven Pines he led a division until the wounding of Gen. Joseph E. Johnston had put him in charge of the army. Within a few hours, however, he would be relieved by General Robert E. Lee. He later feuded with President Davis over a promotion and in disgust, resigned from the regular army on February 17, 1863, having served four days as the acting head of the War Department. Eventually he would be drawn to Joe Brown, with whom he was united in their hatred of President Davis' Administration. Gustavus Smith would accept a Generals commission from the state of Georgia. He took command of the Georgia Militia on June 1, 1864 and within a few weeks they were in action in and around Atlanta.5

General Smith would write, "Governor Brown called into active service the old men of the state up to the age of fifty-five, and the boys down to sixteen years, armed in great part with flint-lock muskets, ordinary rifles, and shot-guns, and ordered them to report to me for service in the field." He would have only two weeks to prepare them for field action before they were pressed into duty.6

A soldier in the Army of Tennessee, Private Sam Watkins

would write of his first impression on seeing the Georgia Militia during the fighting around Atlanta,

> By way of grim jest, and a fitting burlesque
> to tragic scenes, or, rather, to the thing called
> 'glorious war,' old Joe Brown, then Governor of
> Georgia, sent in his militia. It was the richest
> picture of an army I ever saw. It beat
> Forepaugh's double-ringed circus. Every one
> was dressed in citizen's clothes, and the very
> best they had at that time. A few had double-
> barreled shot-guns, but the majority had
> umbrellas and walking sticks, and nearly every
> one had on a duster, a flat-bosomed 'billed'
> shirt, and a plug hat; and, to make the thing more
> ridiculous, the dwarf and the giant were
> marching side by side; the knock-kneed by the
> bow-legged, the driven-in by the side of the
> drawn-out; the pale and sallow dyspeptic, who
> looked like Alex. Stephens, and who seemed to
> have just been taken out of a chimney that
> smoked very badly, and whose diet was goobers
> and sweet potatoes, was placed beside the three
> hundred-pounder, who was dressed up to kill,
> and whose looks seemed to say, 'I've got a
> substitute in the army, and twenty Negroes at
> home besides h-a-a-m, h-a-a-m'.7

In the Atlanta campaign the militia served so well, their performance won the praise of Confederate commander Lt. Gen. John B. Hood, even if it hadn't received the recognition of the regular soldiers of the Army of Tennessee. In his official report of the action around Atlanta, General Hood would add this pertaining to the militia, "This force (Georgia Militia) rendered excellent and gallant service during the siege of Atlanta." During the action around Atlanta the following commands of Georgia State troops also participated: 1st brigade, Brig.-Gen. R. W. Carswell, 2nd brigade, Brig.-Gen. P. J. Phillips, 3rd brigade,

Brig.-Gen. C. D. Anderson and the 4th brigade, Brig.-Gen. H. K.
McCay commanding. The artillery battalion was under the
command of Col C. W. Styles8

After the loss of Atlanta, the Georgia Militia, Augusta and
Athens Battalions, along with the Georgia State Line soldiers,
stayed within the Georgia state boundaries while General Hood
retreated to Alabama. The Georgia troops were given leave by
Governor Joe Brown. They were again called back into service
shortly before the great "March" began. General Smith's troops
stayed near Atlanta where they continually harassed the Union
army stationed in the city. One attack on the Federal lines came
on November 9th, when the Georgia Troops attacked the
enemies works southwest of Atlanta. The Georgian's advanced,
forcing the Union skirmishers back to their inner fortifications.
On this line with plenty of reinforcements to draw from, the
Federals had no trouble beating off the Georgia attackers.
Several Georgians were killed and some of their wounded
relatives and friends had to be left on the field to the enemy
because of the lack of litter bearers. Having to leave these
wounded men on the battlefield must have bothered the militia
and state troops terribly, for it would later explain their actions of
bravery during the fighting at Griswoldville. The Georgia troops
had a total of four months of battle experience in and around
Atlanta before General Sherman's "March to the Sea" began.9

General Smith's Georgians also had gained some battle
experience during Union Cavalry General Stoneman's July 1864
raid into central Georgia in an attempt to release Yankee
prisoners that were being held at Andersonville. General
Stoneman and part of his command had had to surrender to
Confederate Brig. Gen. Alfred Iverson's cavalry near Macon.
Before surrendering, General Stoneman had encountered the
Georgia Militia in a brief, hot skirmish.10

One of the militia's three Brigadier Generals formerly had
served in the Army of Northern Virginia under General Robert E.
Lee. Brig. Gen. Charles D. Anderson had seen action at
Yorktown, Williamsburg, Seven Pines, the Seven Days,
Antietam, Fredericksburg, and Chancellorsville. He was forced

by his wounds to resign on January 20, 1864. He was later commissioned into the Georgia State Militia. Brig. Gen. Henry K. McCay's only experience was in the Georgia Militia. In May 1864 he had been elected lieutenant colonel and during the siege of Atlanta he would be elected brigadier general and assigned to command the newly created 4th Brigade, Georgia Militia. The third brigadier, who would eventually command the militia at Griswoldville, was Brig. Gen. Pleasant J. Phillips. General Phillips' was around 40 years of age as were his fellow militia generals. Phillips was the senior brigadier, but also the least in combat experience. His seniority resulted from his having been a militia officer throughout the war. His only battle experience had been the four months of action around Atlanta the summer of 1864.11

General Smith's command, stationed a short distance outside of Atlanta, were the only infantry force between the union army and the port city of Savannah when General Sherman began his 190 mile march to the sea.12

On October 22, General Wheeler who had been with General Hood's retreat into Alabama was ordered to return to Georgia to watch General Sherman. General Wheeler was left in north Georgia with some 4,500 horsemen and instructions to follow Sherman wherever he might go. Wheeler had close to 2,000 horsemen brought back from his Tennessee raid. He was given Martin's division consisting of Iverson's and Morgan's Brigades. Before November 1, Wheeler would be rejoined with William's Division and Drible's Brigade who had failed to return to Wheeler from Tennessee in early September. Drible's Brigade was much under strengthen at this time in the war. As Hood advanced into Tennessee he would rely solely on General Bedford Forrest to be the Army of Tennessee's eyes and ears.13

When General Wheeler and his command arrived at Jonesboro on November 13, he was informed by an escaped Southern prisoner that there was a great deal of activity on the Western and Atlantic Railroad, primarily men and material moving from Atlanta. From Union captives he then learned that General Sherman had indeed returned to Atlanta and that his troops were being readied for a move to Augusta or Savannah and that the railroad was being destroyed before their departure.[14]

Early on November 15th, General Wheeler found out that there had been extensive destruction in Rome, Marietta, and Atlanta. His scouts brought word later in the day of a mass exodus of infantry, cavalry, artillery and wagons moving south on the McDonough Road from Atlanta.[15]

Brigadier General Judson Kilpatrick's 3rd Union Cavalry Division led the Union right wing from Atlanta to protect the flank from expected Confederate resistance from Macon. They pulled out of East Point on November 15, 1864, with more than 5,000 cavalry and six guns and proceeded to follow the west bank of the Flint River. Their assignment from General Sherman was to feint on the city of Forsyth and try and deceive the Confederate forces into believing Macon was the Union armies first objective of the march.[16]

Both cavalry commanders, Wheeler and Kilpatrick, were well acquainted with each other. They had been classmates at West Point. Wheeler graduated in 1860 and Kilpatrick in 1861. General Judson Kilpatrick shared General Joe Wheeler's recklessness in battle and the clashes between the two cavalry forces would provide most of the military action during the "March to the Sea". Their engagements would be a slashing, vicious series of combats with no quarter given on either side and reports of considerable atrocities committed by all.[17]

Many Georgians were less than happy at the return to their soil of General Wheeler's unruly troopers. While ferocious in action, they were notoriously lacking in discipline. Complaints about his men multiplied from the very Georgia citizens they were there to protect. One Georgian told a Federal soldier, "they are the meanest set of men that ever lived." If that Union soldier had ever been in action against Wheeler's cavalry, I'm sure he nodded in agreement. Some Southern citizens referred to the notorious Confederate calvary as "Wheeler's horse thieves."[18]

Others in the South , during this campaign, would feel differently of the effort made by General Wheeler's outnumbered cavalry force to impede the advance of General Sherman's army.

It was the fortune of war that these horsemen
from Kentucky, Tennessee, (Alabama) and other
States should defend the soil of South Carolina,
(Georgia) from the torch and sword of a ruthless
enemy. Whether this service be considered good
or ill, the patriotism of these men and their
devotion to the cause for which they were
fighting cannot be questioned; for they were
veterans who had followed the failing fortunes
of the Confederacy from Kentucky to the
Carolinas, many of them literally passing by the
doors of their homes in other States. And the
hardships and dangers they encountered should
not be regarded lightly; for when the end came,
their depleted ranks gave evidence that,
"While some gave much and lived,
Others gave all and died."[19]

General Joe Wheelers's first engagement of this campaign
was on November 15, 1864, at Jonesboro, when a superior
number of General Kilpatrick's cavalry drove him from the town
in an early fight at 7:00 a.m. Alabama troops, parts of 2nd,
53rd, 56th Cavalry Regiments of the 24th Battalion, Inge's,
Perrins's and Miller's regiments, suffered a loss of five troopers
and inflicted 40 casualties on the Union cavalry before retreating
back to the militia lines at Lovejoy Station, some six miles south
of Jonesboro. Here the cavalry joined the Georgia Militia and
the other Georgia troops occupying the old earthworks.[20]

One of Wheeler's cavalrymen, Captain William Lewis Nugent
of the 28th Mississippi Cavalry, Ferguson's Brigade, would take
this time to write to his wife Nellie. In his letter he would tell her
of the absence of morals among the women of Georgia, which he
felt was a result of the destitution of the people of the region.
Defeat was unthinkable for Captain Nugent for it meant the
destruction of the planter class of which he was a part of and the
abandonment of the lands to "the freed negroes & the wild
beasts."[21]

4   Skirmish at Lovejoy Station

With the arrival of the Confederate Cavalry at Lovejoy Station on November 16, and the Union cavalry in hot pursuit, the militia knew their wait was over. "Hurricane Sherman" was now blowing their way.

The Federal Troopers, chasing General Wheeler's cavalry, were part of General Kilpatrick's command. A Union battery attached to the cavalry immediately unlimbered and fired a salvo into the Southern position. Then the Federal cavalry dismounted and charged the earthworks.[1] There was a short fight with the small force of General Wheeler's Cavalry of Col. James Hagan's Alabama Brigade and General Smith's Georgia infantrymen. The Confederate cavalry suffered 38 casualties before they mounted and withdrew to Bear Creek leaving the Georgia infantry to fend for themselves.[2]

General Smith had hoped to fight a delaying action from the works built at Lovejoy Station. On learning that the main Union force had turned southeast at Morrow's Station, which now made his position untenable, Smith made plans for a hasty withdrawal.[3]

The Georgians had suffered a few casualties at Lovejoy Station before their quick withdrawal to Hampton, Georgia. More embarrassing for General Smith was the capture of 30 of his men, three caissons loaded with artillery ammunition and two three-inched rifled guns that had been left on the field. The Georgians had proudly captured these same guns in July during the Union raid by General Stoneman's cavalry near Macon. Also 500 Confederate muskets were left scattered about the entrenchments at Lovejoy Station. They had been thrown there by the fleeing Georgian's in their hasty desire to get away from the slashing Federal cavalrymen. Almost one out of every five militiamen in the battle had left their muskets behind during the skirmish.4

Color-bearer Pvt. Christopher Bier from Athens, Company A, of the Athens Battalion, managed to bring the unit's colors back with him from the rout at Lovejoy station. In the Confederate army as well as the Union army it was an honor to be chosen to carry the colors. A soldier had to earn the honor and Pvt. Christopher Bier was indeed proud to bear his unit's colors in action.5

One Georgia Militiaman wrote, "We were so completely run over that we scattered in every direction, those of us who were not killed or captured." This was not what the Georgia troops wanted their friends, relatives and fellow citizens of Georgia, to read about in their daily newspapers. They had endured the derision from the press about being Joe Brown's " pets." They had wanted to show their fellow Georgians that they too were soldiers and could fight as well as the regular army. The militia had indeed fought at Lovejoy Station, but not very well.6

Captain John J. McArthur's Company C, 7th Regiment from Montgomery County, didn't suffer any casualties at Lovejoy Station, but the 27 men in the company had skedaddled along with the rest of the Georgia troops. 7

Retreating with the Georgia troops was the overall commander, Major General Howell Cobb. Cobb nominally in charge of the reserves in Macon rode along with the dispirited troops.8

Militiaman William Dickey managed to grab his blanket, canteen, cartridge belt, knapsack before retreating with his company of fellow Georgians.

The Federal's had suffered only 30 casualties in the short, sharp action at Lovejoy Station. 9

5 Let all of her sons come to her rescue.

Over the next few days a series of correspondences whipped back and fourth from officials in Georgia to Gen. P. G. T. Beauregard, who commanded the Military District of the West, in Corinth, Mississippi, Lt. Gen. R. Taylor in Selma, Alabama, the government in Richmond and even to the commander of the Army of Tennessee who was now located in Tuscumbia, Alabama.

On November 16th, 1864. General Beauregard to General Taylor, "Should you move into Georgia, as referred to in to-day's telegram, don't take troops intended to protect Corinth and Mobile and Ohio Railroad, but hurry them forward soon as possible.[1]

On November 17th, General Beauregard to Governor J. E. Brown, "General R. Taylor has been ordered to take command forthwith of all Confederate troops in Georgia in the limits of Hood's department operating against Sherman."[2]

On November 17th a telegraph from General Beauregards headquarters in Corinth to General Hood, "General, General Beauregard directs me to say that he desires you will take the offensive at the earliest practicable moment and deal the enemy rapid and vigorous blows, striking him while thus dispersed, and by this means distract General Sherman's advance into Georgia..."[3]

General Hood fired back his answer to General Beauregard the same day, "I have just received your letter of this morning. Please inform General Beauregard that I will move at the earliest possible moment and will telegraph him when we start."[4]

The South hoped by unleashing General Hood and his Army of Tennessee, it would cause General Sherman to reverse his army and again chase after them. But it was too late. General

Thomas, in Nashville was now indeed strong enough to face General Hood's army. It would take a major calamity for General Sherman to even consider turning his army around. General Sherman did receive an extra added bonus from his March to the Sea. General Hood was forced to move into Tennessee, before he was totally ready to begin his campaign. As we can see from a November 17, 1864, telegram from General Hood to General Beauregard, "I have now seven days' rations on hand and need thirteen days' additional. Please use every effort to have these supplies pressed forward."[5]

General Beauregard forwarded to General Hood a telegram he had received from General Cobb in Georgia on November 15th. General Hood received it on the 17th. "The enemy has burnt Atlanta and destroyed railroad to Allatoona, burning bridge over Chattahoochee. He moved out of Atlanta with a very large force in the direction of Macon by Jonesborough and McDonough. We have no force to oppose him and must fall back to Macon, where re-inforcements should be sent at once to meet him successfully."

But this late in the war, the only thing the South could send Georgia as it prepared for Hurricane Sherman was a handful of infantry, Wheeler's command and telegrams, and the telegrams kept coming.[6]

Cavalry commander General Wheeler, now in Jonesborough, was notified of General Taylors appointment on November 17th: "General R. Taylor will take command in person forthwith of all Confederate troops in Georgia....do all in your power to check General Shermans advance."[7]

General Beauregard was busy trying to scrape up some troops from the other Southern states for the relief of Georgia, but the South was hitting the bottom of its manpower barrel. The Generals and politicians talked of landing blows and leading troops against the enemy but there weren't any sizable relief available to be sent. In a telegram to Gen. Howell Cobb in Georgia he says,

Have ordered General Taylor to send at once

all troops he can possibly spare, and General
Hood to send immediately one brigade Jackson's
division cavalry, or the whole division if it can
possibly be spared at this juncture. A victory in
Tennessee will relieve Georgia. Call on every
available white man and slave to destroy and
block up roads in General Shermans front,
flanks, and rear.[8]

General Sherman's feint to Macon by General Howard's right
wing was working, but Richmond also had no additional troops
to send to Georgia's aid. On November 17th, Gen.Howell Cobb,
commander of state troops in Macon, wired President Jefferson
Davis in Richmond, asking that the garrisons stationed in
Charleston, Savannah, and Augusta, and re-inforcements from
General Hood's army, be concentrated to defend Macon.
"Sherman's move upon this place is formidable," he wrote, "and
the most dangerous of the war. His policy is universal
destruction." General Cobb believed by concentrating all
available forces in the region, General Sherman could be
defeated, with "the greatest result of the war."[9]

On the same day, former Confederate Secretary of State,
Robert Toombs, who had served with the Army of Northern
Virginia through March, 1863, became concerned with the
situation in Georgia. At Antietam it was Robert Toombs' gallant
small band of Georgians that had held the Union 9th Corps in
check at the bridge. Toombs now strictly a political General,
wired Governor Brown from Macon, "Things are very bad here,
Let all of her sons come to her rescue," Toombs would
proclaim.[10]

By November 18, 1864 even if the South could scrape enough
troops together to assist Georgia, it would have been too late to
transport them to where they were needed to stop the Northern
army. General Sherman's march to the sea was already in its
third full day.

Both General Beauregard and General Taylor were en route to

Macon Georgia by November 18th, to meet with Gen. Howell Cobb and Governor Joe Brown.

On November 18th General Hardee was put in temporary command of all troops in Georgia, until the arrival of General Taylor. On this day General Cobb received a dispatch from President Davis, directing him to obstruct the roads.[11]

General Beauregard, bombarded from Georgia with telegraphs for help, started to vacillate. Originally he wanted to start General Hood north into Tennessee as soon as possible, but now fired a wire to Governor Isham G. Harris in Florence, Alabama, "I have left it optional with General Hood to divide and re-enforce General Cobb, or take offensive to relieve him and Georgia."[12]

An appeal had even been issued from the Confederate capitol at Richmond, from former Georgia Senator B. H. Hill, exhorting his fellow Georgian's. It read,

> To the People of Georgia:
> You have now the best opportunity ever
> yet presented to destroy the enemy. Put
> everything at the disposal of our generals;
> remove all provisions from the path of the
> invader, and put all obstructions in his path.
> Every citizen with his gun, and every
> Negro with his spade and hoe can do the work of
> a soldier. You can destroy the enemy by
> retarding his march.
> Georgians, be firm! Act promptly, and
> fear not![13]

Governor Joe Brown who in the short interval between the succession of Georgia and the formation of the Confederacy, enjoyed the distinction of being the chief executive of the sovereign and independent republic of Georgia, released a proclamation to the citizens of Georgia from Milledgeville on November 19, 1864,

The whole people understand how imminent is the danger that threatens the state. Our cities are being burned, our fields laid waste, and our wives and children mercilessly driven from their homes by a powerful enemy. We must strike like men for freedom or we must submit to subjugation.

Death is to be preferred to loss of liberty. All must rally to the field for the present emergency or the state is over run.

I therefore by virtue of the authority vested in me by the statute of this state, hereby order a levy (en masse) of the whole free white population residing or domiciled in this state between sixteen and fifty-five years of age, except such as are physically unable to bear arms, which physical defect must be plain and indisputable, or they must be sent to camp for examination, and except those engaged in the legislature or judicial departments of the government, which are by the recent act of the lesgislatrue declared exempt from compulsory service.

All others are absolutely required, and members of the legislature and judges are invited to report immediately to Major G.A. Smith, at Macon or wherever else in Georgia his camp may be, for forty (40) days service under arms, unless the emergency is sooner passed.

The statute declares that all persons hereby called out shall be subject after this call to all rules and articles of war of the Confederate States, and on failure to report, shall be subject to the pains and penalties of the crime of desertion.

Volunteer organizations formed into companies, battalions, regiments, brigades,

brigades or divisions will be accepted for (40) forty days, if they even approximate to the numbers in each organization which is required by the militia, laws of this state which were in force prior to the late act. All police companies formed in counties for home defense will report leaving at home for the time, only those over 55 years of age; and all persons having Confederate deferrals or exemptions, who by the late decision of the supreme court of this state, are held to be able to state militia service and bound to obey the call of the Governor.

All such refusing to report will be arrested by the police force or by any aid de camp, or other officer of this state, and carried immediately to the front. The necessary employees of rail roads now actively engaged, and the necessary agents of the express company, and telegraph operators are from necessity for their services in their present positions, excused.

All ordained ministers of religion in charge of a church or synagogue are also excused.

All railroad companies in this state will transport all persons applying for transportation to the front, and in case anyone refuses, its president, superintendent, agents and employees will be immediately sent to the front.

All aids de camp and other state officials are requested to be active and vigilant in the execution of the orders contained in this proclamation, and all Confederate officers are respectfully invited to aid state officers in their vicinity in sending forward all persons as hereby ordered to the front.

The enemy has penetrated almost to

the center of your state. If every Georgian able to
bear arms would rally around him, he could
never escape.
Signed:Joseph E. Brown, Governor.14

Governor Brown's earlier conscription exemptions in Georgia
had created resentment from soldiers in the regular army. A
soldier would write in his journal that during an address made to
a gathering of regular troops of Hood's Army of Tennessee in
Gadsden, Alabama, on October 21, Confederate General Bate
made light of the sorghum exemption. He had criticized
Governor Brown's action in an impromptu parody to Campbell's
downfall of Poland,

What tho' destruction sweep these lovely plains,
Who cares for liberty while sorghum yet remains?
With that sweet name we wave our knives on high,
And swear to cut it while we live and suck it till we die.
15

Few would or even could heed this clarion call to arms of
Governor Joe Brown. It wasn't that Georgia was growing callous
towards the war, there just wasn't any available man power left in
the state. Thousands of Georgians were serving gallantly under
Gen. Lee in Virginia. 3,311 Georgians had become casualties
during the Battle of Gettysburg campaign alone. Georgians were
also serving with distinction in Gen. Hood's Army of Tennessee.
The best estimate that can be made of troops Georgia furnished,
first and last, to the Confederate Army is between 120,000 and
125,000 men. Many of the South's leading generals hailed from
the state of Georgia. Georgia had given to the Southern cause till
it hurt.
There were a few Southern men who were clever enough to
avoid service altogether. There was one young man who never
hid from a guard sent out to find him. He merely sat on his front
porch in a rocking chair, dressed as a woman, and when the
soldiers appeared he would send them off on a wild goose chase

by giving false directions in a high, squeaky voice. But most men and even a few women stepped forward to do their duty and serve in the Confederate Army[16]

General John Bell Hood finally got his Army of Tennessee moving north on Monday, November 21, 1864. His proclamation to the army issued that day had boldly announced: "You march today to redeem by your valor one of the fairest portions of our Confederacy. This can only be achieved by battle and by victory." His field orders for the campaign urged "a cheerful, manly spirit" and "determined patriotism" in meeting the expected hardships as they marched to repossess the "fruitful fields of Tennessee."[17]

Meanwhile the fruitful fields of Georgia were being laid to waste as General Sherman's Legion was cutting a 40 mile desolate swath across the central part of the state heading east to the sea.

On November 18th General Beauregard realizing he had not been able to assist with much in the way of reinforcements tried to exhort the people of Georgia with a statement,

> To the people of Georgia:
> Arise for the defense of your native soil!
> Rally around your patriotic Governor and gallant
> soldiers. Obstruct and destroy all the roads in
> Sherman's front, flank, and rear, and his army
> will soon starve in your midst. Be confident. Be
> resolute. Trust in an overruling Providence, and
> success will soon crown your efforts. I hasten to
> join you in the defense of your homes and
> firesides.
> G. T. Beauregard

6 Ceaseless War
God Help Us

After the defeat at Lovejoy Station earlier in the day, the Redding brothers, Pvts. William and James, trudged along with the rest of the dispirited militia back to Hampton, Georgia. Hampton was located halfway between Atlanta and Griffin, about 45 miles north-west of Macon. As the Georgians marched, the dust from the clay roads clung to their heavy cotton uniforms. Some 500 of the soldiers didn't even have a weapon after they had flung them to the ground before hastily departing the defenses at Lovejoy Station.[1]

Major Jackson's Augusta Battalion was also a dispirited group as they moved along the road to Hampton. Captain Holleyman, Company A commander, marched with his men who all hailed from Augusta. He was joined in the march by Lieutenant Meyers, Pvts. John Copeland, William Churchill, Simeon Buford and the others of Colonel Jackson's Augusta Battalion. The noise of their weapons, canteens and accountrements banged together as they moved along the dusty road.

The remaining 27 men and boys of Capt. John J. McArthur's Company C, 7th Regiment, from Montgomery County, couldn't be too happy with their and the other Georgia troops performance in the previous fight, as they marched back to Hampton. Their only consolation was that no one in the company had been killed in the action.

When the Georgian troops finally did arrive at Hampton, they immediately began erecting a barricade across the road to Atlanta. Sgt. Blanton Nance Company E joined the others of his 7th Regiment, Georgia Militia, in tearing up fences and whatever else could be found to pile on, as if by making it bigger it would in itself keep the enemy cavalry back. Company E commander, Captain Morgan, got his men in behind the barricade along with the rest of the Georgia troops, settled in and waited.2

At noon Colonel Hagan's brigade of General Wheeler's cavalry, again Inge's, Perrin's and Miller's Regiments from Alabama, came dashing into the Hampton lines recently completed by the Georgia troops. The cavalry dismounted, grabbed their weapons and joined the Georgians at the roadblock. They just had time to man the barricades when General Kilpatrick's Union cavalry swept up to the Confederate defensive line. With a burst of musket fire another sharp fight ensued before the Federal cavalry again overwhelmed the Georgia position. Twenty additional prisoners, again mostly Georgia infantrymen, were captured by General Kilpatrick's cavalry. During this engagement there were no reports of large groups of men throwing their weapons down and "skedaddling." At Hampton the Georgia troops of General Smith's command had held on to their weapons and although giving ground and falling back, would live to fight again. The Alabama cavalrymen lost eight in the skirmish for control of the roadblock. The Federal cavalry lost 50 before the Southerners picked up in the dark and this time retreated some 15 miles back to already prepared works at Griffin, Georgia. The Georgia troops from General Smith's command would arrive after a hard march, at 1:00 a.m. in the morning, footsore, tired and hungry, before finally falling into the Grifffin fortifications at Camp Stephens.3

One of the main complaints of the Georgia troops at Camp Stephens, at that time, was the sickness in camp and not of Yankee bullets. Some would complain of just being tired of the war. William Dickey wrote his wife from Griffin, "I am getting tired out with this war, I assure you, worse and worse every day, and there is a great majority in the same fix as myself."4

In the short time he would be at Griffin, Confederate Jonathan Bridges, Company C, 11th Regiment, had time to write his wife Fanny another letter. He still hadn't heard from his wife in three weeks and was still anxious to receive some news from home,

Camp near Griffin, Georgia
November 16, 1864
My Fanny,

I write you a few lines this evening to let you hear from me. I am well only very sore and tired. We had a very hard march last night. We left Lovejoys Station at dark and got to this place at one o'clock last night, 15 miles. We rather skedaddled, I think.

The Yankees is coming on towards Griffin, I suppose. We have orders to cook two days rations. I do not know where we will go to. I think we will go to Macon or Augusta or stay where we are for sometime yet. I have not put on clean clothes but once since I left home and I am very dirty at this time. I can not advise you anything how to do for I have not heard from you in three long mortal weeks and am nearly crazy to hear from you. I write every four, whether you get them or not an I want you to write to me as often as you can. My mess bought 50 lbs. of flour a few days ago and we have biscuits without grease. I tell you they are pretty tuff. I am nearly out of money and then I will have to do without such things as flour, syrup and so forth.

Direct your letters to
Jonathan Bridges
Co. C, 11th Regt.
4th Brigade, Georgia Militia
Macon, Georgia

I see no prospect of coming home in a long while yet. BARNEY is well. I hope you all may be well and doing better than I am though I ought not to complain for I fare better than some of the other soldiers.   Your Jonathan
as ever.5

There was a large Confederate supply and hospital center in Griffin and the Southerners hoped to protect it from capture or destruction by the Federals. The hospital in Griffin was still crowded with the Confederate wounded from the Atlanta campaign.6

On this day General Wheeler identified four Federal Corps and estimated General Sherman's strength at 60,000 to 70,000 men. Sherman's infantrymen were being skillfully shielded by General Kilpatrick's cavalry so much so that General Wheeler continued to report that General Sherman was heading for Macon. Wheeler ordered the roads leading to Macon, Columbus, and Augusta picketed by his cavalry.7

General Wheeler's Alabama cavalry of Hagan's Brigade was in action again, this time, at Bear Creek Station on November 16th. The Ohio Volunteer Calvary of the 2nd Brigade made a saber charge against the Confederate troopers. Lieutenant-Colonel Sanderson led his men into the dismounted Southerners who were posted behind some rail barricades strung out on the road. The Ohioans drove the Southerners back in the ensuing fight losing a total 50 casualties in the charge. They reported capturing 20 Confederates including three commissioned officers from the Alabama brigade. The Alabama cavalrymen reported a loss of only eight casualties in the fight at Bear Creek Station.8

From his headquarters in Griffin, on November 17, 1864, General Wheeler wired General Beauregard, "I have no orders regarding the holding of any city should enemy besiege or assault. Please give me instructions and intentions of Government."9

General Beauregard let General Wheeler know that men were more important than cities. He was ordered to abandoned cities before his men were trapped by a siege. Men were of the main importance at this time in the war. The South had had their share of sieges, Vicksburg, Atlanta, ports up and down the coasts and rivers. Most of them had turned out to be disastrous for the Confederate cause.10

Scout Manson Manley from Spalding County and several

other scouts, who were now stationed in Macon, had been sent
out to see where General Sherman's army was advancing to.
Scout Manley and the other horsemen spent the night of
November 16th, at Sylvan Grove. Manley was surprised to see
his sister Emma Manley and her niece and college mate, Mary
Buttrill and several maids being driven in a wagon by a wounded
Southern soldier, Ben Drake. Mary's brother, Taylor, was also
among the Confederate scouting party. Emma's party had just
arrived at a well at a Stephen Johnson's home, where Manley,
Taylor and the other scouts were watering their horses. Citizens
of Spalding County and all along the Central Railroad's tracks
south of Lovejoy Station were in a state of alarm. Some fled to
Macon and some even beyond to southwest Georgia, trying to get
out of the way of General Sherman's right wing that was
commanded by Gen. O. O. Howard. Emma's parents fearing for
her safety had sent her out of the expected path of the Federals.[11]

Before Emma and her brother could share greetings, they saw
a "blue cloud of Yankee Soldiers coming over the hill." Manson
Manley, Taylor Buttrill and the rest of the Confederate scouts
mounted their horses and dashed off "at a great speed for
Macon."[12]

Quickly a "hundred or more Blue Coats on fast horses came
up" and found Emma, Mary, the driver and their maids at the
well. Emma would later describe what happened next to her
friends. "The Yankee soldiers yelled out, 'Where are those damn
Rebs that were with you?' We said, Gone. Manda, one of the
maids, ran up the road screaming, come back Marse Taylor and
give up. These Yankees will kill you. She mislead them; they
(Union cavalry) ran for miles and came back cursing furiously
for our boys had taken the right hand road to Macon." The
soldiers returned to call her a liar. Emma replied angrily, "Sir,
I'll have you know I am a Southern lady!" As they rode away
with the soldiers, she heard "the rumbling of the great army at a
distance coming."[13, 14]

The Union horsemen took the girls to Gen. George E.
Spencer's tent, commander of the U.S. 1st Alabama Cavalry.
The General then took them to a small log cabin farm house, the

home of a Mrs. Fear. He told Mrs. Fear to take them in "or I'll burn your house damn quick." He then put a guard around the house and according to Emma, personally attended to the girls' needs.15

General Spencer stayed with the girls at the cabin for three hours after the army had passed. He then left them food and gave them a horse to get them home. General Spencer then joined his command.16

On November 17, General Kilpatrick rode from Hampton to the Towliga river to threaten the Georgia cities of Griffin and Forstyth. Part of this Northern force was composed of the 5th Kentucky Cavalry Regiment under the command of Colonel Baldwin. They had earlier been in reserve during the fight at Lovejoy Station. In that position they had seen no action in the fight for the entrenchments. Early on November 17, they had moved out at 7:00 a.m. and advanced about three miles when they were met by a Union Captain Beggs who gave Colonel Baldwin orders to move up the road to attack a brigade of Confederate cavalry. The Southerners were supposed to be encamped along the Towlaliga bridge. Colonel Baldwin followed his orders exactly and charged his regiment the two and a half miles to the bridge only to find a force of perhaps 20 of the enemy left behind to fight a rear guard action against the Federal cavalry. The bridge had been burned and the "rebel camp had been evacuated." Colonel Baldwin would report. At Towaliga bridge the Southern cavalry had lost five of their force of 20 before withdrawing while inflicting 40 casualties on the Union troopers.17

As reported by General Kilpatrick and General Wheeler, the intensity of the fights between the Union and Confederate cavalry on the march was in the same class as the battles of Shiloh, Antietam, Gettysburg and Chickamauga. Both official reports were replete with remarks such as "completely routed" or "flee in uncontrollable confusion." The truth during this campaign was probably some what more in the middle of the claims made by the two opposing commanders.18

At Griffin, General G. W. Smith reported that, "The Federals made serious demonstrations on our lines, but no real attack. Later it was ascertained that a large portion of their forces had passed through McDonough, ten miles or more to the east of us, and were nearer to Macon than we were."[19]

The Union cavalry had indeed moved south-east from Griffin and the threat to that city abated. Capt. Robert H. Barron and Pvt. W. T. Morgan, along with the rest of the Georgia militia, were relieved that there wouldn't be any action at Grifffin. Their commander, General Smith, believed they had helped save Griffin from destruction from the Union force. With the threat to Griffin receding, General G. W. Smith ordered his Georgia troops to now fall back to Forsythe.[20]

The Georgia infantrymen suffered only a few casualties in the skirmishing at Griffin. Private Haralson, Company C, 7th Regiment of Anderson's Brigade would be killed in the action. He wouldn't return to his home county of Montgomery. Company C's roster would now be down to only 26 men with the death of Private Harralson.[21]

William Dickey of the Georgia Militia, in a letter to his wife Anna, described the hardships encountered by the Georgia troops over the last three days,

> (You can not) know the hardships that I have
> passed through in the last three days and nights.
> On the evening of the 15th we got orders to pack
> up and about night we took up a line of march to
> Griffin, arriving at old Camp Stephens about
> 1:30 o'clock pretty well used up. I have written
> you a letter about the march to Camp Stephens
> and put it in the office on Wednesday night.
> That was the 16th, but I don't know that you will
> ever get the letter. On that evening we
> commenced our march to Barnesville.[22]

Sergeant Blanton Nance, Company E, 7th Regiment, Georgia Militia, helped his men pack up their gear, knapsacks, canteens, haversacks and their arms before they joined the rest of the

Georgia soldiers as they moved south toward Forsyth, Georgia. William Brown Henslee of Co. L, 5th Regiment packed his grimy gear and joined the others in line of march. Most of the soldiers hadn't been able to bathe or change clothes since leaving home. They felt and looked dirty. It took them a little under twenty-four hours of marching, mostly in the dark, to reach their thirty-five mile destination, the city of Forsythe. When the Georgians finally arrived they were cold, tired and hungry. It had been a tiring couple of days for the Georgia troops with much more marching then fighting taking place.23

Militiaman William Dickey would continue his letter to his wife of his experiences while in Griffin,

> We come through Griffin after night until about
> one hour today we stopped. After day we started
> again and marched all day until 10 o'clock last
> night. We ate what little we had and could get,
> not having any rations given us since the day
> before, and then did not get it in time to cook it
> and had to throw it away. Grom Griffin (to)
> Forsyth (is) about 40 miles, which we made (in)
> one day and night.24

At Forsythe, the Georgia militia arrived just in time to help repel the advance of General Sherman's Cavalry and save the large depot of supplies from falling into enemy hands. That night General Smith in Forsythe wired Maj.-Gen. Cobb in Macon requesting that enough train cars be sent him for four thousand men. He urged General Cobb to have the trains there before midnight for use by his troops.25

General Kilpatrick later wrote in his report, "After pushing well in on Forsyth and being convinced that the impression had been made upon the enemy our forces were moving directly on that point, I rapidly marched (eastward) to Planter's Factory, crossed the Ocmulgee River and reached Clinton on November 19th." Captain Yates Beebe, commanding Kilpatrick's artillery, said in his report that the march covered some 32 miles and that

10 horses died on the way.26

Colonel Charles Colcock Jones, General Hardee's Chief of Artillery, would comment on the Union armies sweep across Georgia,

> The conduct of Sherman's army and particularly of Kilpatrick's cavalry and the numerous parties swarming through the country in advance and on the flanks of the main columns during the march from Atlanta to the coast, is reprehensible in the extreme....the Federal on every hand and at all points indulged in unwanton pillage, wasting and destroying what could not be used. Defenseless women and children and weak old men were not infrequently driven from their homes, their dwellings fired, and these noncombatants subjected to insult and privation. The inhabitants, white and black, were often robbed of their personal effects, were intimidated by threats-and occasionally were even hung up to the verge of strangulation to compel revelation of the places where money, plate and jewelry were buried, or plantation animals were concealed.27

General Cobb seems to have grasped the full significance of General Sherman's march early on, and saw the only way to stop him. In Macon on November 17th, he wrote to President Jefferson Davis,

> Sherman's move upon this place (Macon) is formidable, and the most dangerous of the war. His policy is universal destruction. If by concentration of all forces that can be brought together Sherman's army could be crushed, he having cut loose from his Communications, it would be the greatest result of the war...If not

beaten here he will march to Charleston, Savannah.[28]

It was late on the night of November 17 when Confederate General G. W. Smith finally received some of the trains he had earlier requested. Loading only half his force on the trains that night, he sent them on to Macon. Not receiving all the trains he needed to move his full force, he delayed the departure of the remainder of his command and fourteen pieces of artillery until the following morning. Some Georgians were just too worn out to board the cars and move off to Macon. [29]

Militiaman William Dickey would write his wife Anna about his short stay in Forsyth,

> But, as I was going to say, we had all got to sleep last night about 11 o'clock and was roused up about 12 and ordered into line and marched up to the depot at Forsyth and took the train for this place and arrived here (Macon) about sunrise this morning. I have not slept three hours in two days and nights all put together.[30]

Captain McArthur's 25 men of Company C, 7th Regiment, Georgia Militia, boarded the trains that morning with the rest of the Georgia soldiers. They would join their comrades already in Macon.[31]

In Macon, General Cobb found himself in a desperate situation. To protect this important industrial center, which he considered Sherman's main target, Cobb had no more than a handful of convalescents and reserves.[32]

Union Private Dozer, 26th Illinois Infantry, would write in his diary of the days actions,

> Nov 17th 1864. Thursday. Pleasant We started at sunrise (the forage detail party) from Mcdonnel (McDonough) and got in front of the troops. About 2 miles from town We come

across a fine lot of Hogs of which we killed one
dozin of ... then kept in the road until we
camped. Marching near Indian Springs.33

Colonel Oscar L. Jackson of the 63rd Ohio Regiment, wrote
in his diary of the days activities of November 17,

We had only an hour and a half last night to get
supper and get breakfast this morning. Have
been fifty-eight hours out of Atlanta, forty-four
of which we passed on the road with knapsacks.
Pretty severe campaigning, but sweet potatoes
are plenty and we do better.34

On November 18, when the remainder of Gen. G. W. Smith's
command began to trickle into Macon, after the delay of a lack of
transportation, he turned over all of his force except the Georgia
Militia and two regiments of State Line troops to General Cobb.
General Cobb then issued orders for General Smith's troops to be
assigned to the defense of a portion of the line around Macon
which was located on the west bank of the Ocmulgee River.35
    The fourteen pieces of artillery would arrive on the last train
from Forsythe.36 General Smith would later write how he had
acquired Anderson's Battery for his command during the fight
for Atlanta the previous summer.

Fortunately for this small body of militia,
there was then in Atlanta a Confederate battery
of light pieces, commanded by Captain
Anderson. That battery had just been refitted for
field service, and was awaiting orders to return
to the front. Without other authority than my
own, but with the full consent of the officers and
men, I took this battery with the militia when we
crossed the Chattahoochee at Jame's Ferry, and
assumed position in the open country, within
close supporting distance of our small force of

cavalry, five or six miles from the left of General
Johnston's intrenched position.

With the artilleries arrival, Captain Anderson's Battery of 12-
pounder Gun-Howitzer's, nicknamed the "Napoleon", was put in
position outside of Macon with General Smith's militia, Athens,
Augusta troops and the Georgia State Line men. Other troops
made up of Macon city clerks, a few volunteers and less
wounded convalescent soldiers from the hospital in the city
would also man the fortifications.37

The "Napoleon" was the work-horse cannon for both sides
throughout the conflict. Cast in 6-pounder caliber this light,
durable smooth bore weapon had a range of 2,000 yards and
hurled more solid shot, case shot, grape and canister than all the
other ordnance combined. It was a simple piece, cast of bronze
or iron, and mounted on an iron-bound wooden carriage on
which was carried its own rammer, sponge, leather grease bucket
and rope for hauling. Behind it stood its limber, just an
ammunition chest on wheels, and to which the piece was attached
when pulled by its 6-horse team.

From Macon General Smith would report,

> The face of the country was open, the roads
> were in good order, the weather was fine and
> bracing , the crops had been gathered, and were
> ready for use; in short, a combination of
> circumstances favored an easy march for General
> Sherman's army. It was evidently no part of his
> purpose to attack fortified places in the interior
> of the state. He was only passing through it to
> his ultimate destination-subsisting on the country
> along his route, and destroying a great deal of
> property, besides throughly breaking up the
> railroads, thus cutting off communications
> between Richmond and the States of Alabama,
> Mississippi, Louisiana, and Florida.38

General Wheeler's instructions from General Beauregard were to impede the enemy's advance in any possible manner and attack isolated Federal troops and foragers. The plan was to try and keep the destruction of the Union army to a limited, narrow track. His men were to harass the Federal rear and burn supply wagons. General Wheeler was also expected to be the eyes and ears for the officials now gathering in Macon. Much of his time was spent on dispatches to his superiors. He was also ordered to give civilians living along the route of General Sherman's march at least a day's notice of the enemy's arrival, so they could either leave or hide their valuables. All of these extra added duties would further deplete his already weak cavalry force. The officials in Macon told Wheeler that a scorched earth policy was not to be followed, private property was not to be burned by his cavalry force.39

General Joseph Wheeler's Alabama cavalry had been in action almost continuously since General Sherman had left Atlanta, fought again, this time in an engagement at Runs Creek on November 18th. In the action the Confederate calvary lost four men to the Federal cavalry loss of 24 casualties. It was a short, sharp engagement of crackling rifles and flashing sabers that seemed to characterize these meetings between the two opposing cavalries. The Confederate cavalry, like the Georgia infantrymen, would eventually fall back to the safety of the defenses around Macon.40

On that day Union soldiers captured a batch of Confederate mail. Several of the letters expressed the belief that General Sherman intended to advance through Augusta. Sherman's feint on Macon was working.41

Major Henry Hitchcock of General Sherman's staff would write that during the day "some of our stragglers were shot by citizens or scouts." He would add, "served them right." Major Hitchcock had become alarmed by the looting of the Georgia homes.42

Private Dozer of the 26th Illinois Infantry would write of the days events in his diary,

November 18th 1864. Friday warm We
started in front of the Brig at 7 in the morning.
We got in camp last night at 10 oc(lock) We
marched to Indian Springs in front of Brig where
we stopped till they came up we got some forage
at Indian Springs...where we camped for the
night.[43]

Also at Indian Springs on November 18, was the 100th
Indiana infantryman, Private Theodore Upson,

This has been a summer resort and there is a
low long building here called the Hotel. I think
there must be some 250 rooms in it. No one
lives in it. Our boys rummaged around and
found a chest with a lot of silver coin and a bag
filled with ivory poker chips. I have a few of
them I shall keep as souvenirs. I had been quite
sick for a day before we got here, all on account
of those flap jacks and felt so bad that Captain
Fobes said I had better go to a house close by
and stay till we moved. The old man who
owned the house took my canteen and got me
some water out of a mineral spring which soon
fixed me up, and now I feel all right. There are a
great many mineral springs here and all seem to
be different kinds of water.[44]

On the retrograde back to Macon, at Ulcofaw, the Alabama
cavalry had another run in with the Union cavalry. Colonel
Hagan's units of Inge's, Perrin's, and Miller's regiments inflicted
39 casualties on the enemy while suffering only two lost.
Although almost always outnumbered in these short and violent
cavalry engagements, their sudden hit and run tactics were
beginning to take a toll on the Union calvary.[45]
General Wheeler and his force finally pulled back into the
lines at Macon at 11 p.m. November 19th, where he found Lt.

Gen. William J. Hardee had been appointed as the new commander of the Department of South Carolina, Georgia, and Florida. Even as the Souther cavalry arrived the Union cavalry were nipping at their heels. In five days of continuous running fights with General Kilpatrick's cavalry, Hagan's Alabama troopers had fought six battles, suffered 62 casualties and inflicted 193 casualties on the Federals. Just as General Wheeler's cavalry was riding into the fortifications outside Macon, hundreds of frightened citizens of that city were crowding onto trains heading south to the safety of Albany, Georgia.[46]

The city, and indeed the whole of middle Georgia, was in a state of anxiety. Nevertheless most of the people had a determination to withstand if possible and, if not, to endure whatever fate was in store for them. "This is no time for weak and timid men," the *Macon Telegraph and News* would write. "He who thinks of fleeing at the approach of his adversary is unworthy of the name of man."[47]

Among those leaving on the outward bound trains were Gen. Joseph E. Johnston and his wife. Formerly commander of the Confederate Army of Tennessee, General Johnston had made Macon his home since his removal from command in July 1864.[48]

When Georgia became an independent republic on January 19, 1861, the city of Macon had celebrated heartily. The *Macon Telegraph and News* would report on January 22, the "City was one sea of light."[49] Like most Southern cities, Macon was now suffering the effects of three years of war. Slavery, inflation and shortage of certain materials were some of the evils of the war, as sheeting went to $5 per yard, corn meal from $3 to $5 per bushel, and the universal coffee was parched acorns, corn or peas. A batch of money would buy little. A rich man normally could eat a feast for $5 but now that much money would only buy you a pauper's meal. A two page newspaper cost $2 in Confederate money, yet 5 cents in specie. Confederate gold dollars in 1861 worth 90 cents dropped to only 6 cents in 1864.[50]

Salt also became a very scarce item in Macon and elsewhere

in the south. It was mined and prepared in the North, who had cut off all the supply, as well as blockading all the Southern seaports. So the South was even lacking the most common article of all, salt.[51]

The South, because of the blockade, even lacked the basic medicines to treat her children. One heart-broken woman wrote to her husband serving in the Confederacy, "Twenty grains of quinine would have saved our two children. They were too nauseated to drink the bitter willow tea, and they are now at rest, and I have no one to work for but you. Do not think of coming. I am well and strong, and am not dismayed. I think day and night of your sorrow. I have their little graves near me."[52]

The area General Sherman left behind was naturally the most destitute. Mary A. H. Gay, a DeKalb County resident, kept a diary of the extreme hardships of this ravaged land. She told of spending a whole day picking grains of corn out of bureau drawers and other improvised troughs the Federal had used for feeding their horses. Her labor yielded about half a bushel of grain. From this corn meal she made mush and hotcakes to ward of starvation. In the bitter cold of November 1864, Mrs. Gay gathered scrap metal from the battlefield of Atlanta and exchanged the metal at the Confederate commissary for much-needed food.[53]

Not all the civilians had left the central Georgia cities or even escaped being in the path of the Union army as it rolled to the sea. While their husbands and sons were in the service, some wives and families of the Georgia soldiers stayed and fought back with the only weapons they could muster, their indomitable spirits that would not break.[54]

In a quiet reply to abusive comments made by Union soldiers who had stripped her farm of almost everything, while her frighted children watched on, the Southern woman said, "Our men will fight you as long as they live." Then gesturing to her children she added, "and these boy'll fight you when they grow up."[55]

Another woman, a proud wife to a Confederate Captain away in service, defiantly said, "take everything we have, I can live on pine straw the rest of my days. You can kill us, but you can't conquer us."[56]

One woman was asked by Union troops if her husband had been drafted into Confederate service. She spat before she replied, "I wouldn't have a man if he had to be conscripted."[57]

When General Sherman's troops entered Milledgeville, a young girl, Anna Maria Greene, would record in her diary the following note, "We went through the house singing 'We live and die with Davis.'"[58]

Twenty-year old Anna Maria Green lived in Milledgeville, where her father served as superintendent of the state asylum for the mentally ill would write,

> Saturday evening November 19th-Again we are in a state of excitement caused by the near approach to our town of the enemy. Last night they were two thousand strong at Monticello. Cobb having ordered the cadets and other troops we had for local defense to Macon there to meet the yankees. Governor Brown ordered the evacuation of Milledgeville, and today has been one of intense excitement, families moving and the cadets and the other troops...no train arrived.[59]

Mary Gay of Decatur would say, "If I were a man, I should be in the foremost ranks of those who are fighting for rights guaranteed by the Constitution of the United States."[60]

Nothing would anger the Southern women more than the fact that Northern women were encouraging their men to bring back treasures from the South. Kate Cumming recorded in her journal that letters found on dead Union soldiers on the battlefields contained, "Petitions from the women to send them valuables from the South. One says she wants a silk dress, another a watch, and one writer told her husband that now was the time to get a piano, as they could not afford to buy one."[61]

But war weariness at home, as well as on the battlefields that were strewn with dead and dying, sometimes caused a break in morale. Maryann Mosely of Macon would write to her son William begging him to come home "a Christmas." She didn't want him "to go to the Confederate army." But there were more Georgia women who were dominated by their fighting spirit and who held their men loyal to the cause than there were of the other kind.[62]

Union private, Jesse Dozer, 26th Illinois Infantry, would write of today's events in his diary,
"19th Saturday. Warm & rainy We started at 6 o'clock & got in front of the Division...We went to camp with our forage. The Regt. was on the road until 3 o'clock in the morning."[63]

Private Upson's 100th Indiana Infantry Regiment was also on the march on November 19, when the weather turned bad. They began the march on this day at 10 a.m., crossing the Ocmulgee river on a pontoon bridge, advanced some 15 miles "through the rain and over the worst of roads" a report would read. The 100th Indiana Infantry would eventually encamp at 2 a.m. on the Hillsbough road.[64]

The Union army continued to forage the countryside heavily as they moved eastward. One Northern officer Maj. Henry Hitchcock, who was new to General Sherman's staff and handled his correspondence, was bothered by the excesses that had so far attended the foraging. He wrote,

> Either we must acknowledge the 'C.S.A.' or we must conquer them: to conquer we must make war, and it must be war, it must bring destruction and desolation, it must make the innocent suffer as well as the guilty, it must involve plundering, burning, killing. Else it is worse than a sham. Shall we then quit and acknowledge the C.S.A.? No, for that is simply to ensure the same thing hereafter, for separation means ceaseless war, God help us![65]

On Sunday morning, November 20, 1864, after a restless

sleep, General G. W. Smith's Georgians, were up early and
began manning the trenches and strong points located on the
outskirts of the city of Macon. Thirteen year old Pvt. Bridges
Smith and fourteen year old Pvt. W. A. Poe of the 5th Regiment,
Georgia Militia, both from Macon, shuffled along in a dense
morning fog to man a series of rifle pits and cannon
emplacements located in the redoubts on the rim of the city.
These fortifications had been prepared earlier for the defense of
Macon. Private William Caswell, the litter bearer Company H,
5th Regiment, would man these defenses with the rest of General
Smith's command along with some cavalry, convalescents, and a
few local men who had heeded the clarion call "to arms" to
defend their city.[66]

From Macon militiaman William Dickey would pen this letter
to his wife,

> Macon, Georgia : November 18, 1864
> My dearest Anna: You will perceive by the
> heading of this letter that I am in Macon again.
> We arrived this morning about sunup from
> Forsyth....This morning I thought I would fall
> out and come up here and get a warm breakfast
> (at the Brown House hotel). I was just in the
> humor for it, I assure you, and done it justice.
> After eating breakfast, I thought I would write to
> you and let you know how we all are. We were
> all used Completely up. Bill Heir and Brother
> Henry come through. They are well, all except
> being used up by the march. Pat McGriff has
> been complaining, but is better now than he was.
> Several of our boys are left behind broke down.
> They did not come up in time to take the train
> with us this morning, but I hope they will all
> come through safe....The fear (of) being captured
> made them stand up so well. They marched in
> pain and misery, I assure you. I kept up with the
> command all the time but done it by hard work

and lots of pain. I thought my feet would burn up. I never traveled in as much pain and soreness in my life. I don't think any troops ever marched as hard before. The times looks gloomy about here now, I assure you. The citizens of Macon are in great confusion and are moving out Pretty fast. It is not worthwhile for me to write you anything about the Yankees, as you will know as much as I can tell you and sooner than I can tell you. Suffice it to say they are making demonstrations this way. The hopes that we had of being let loose soon has faded from our minds at this time. I can't say what will be the next move on foot or whether we will stay here long or not. I will not be surprised at any move now. We may have to retreat from this place. You can direct your letters as before to Griffin. They will stop here anyhow. I will try and (notify you) if there is any change. I received a letter from (you) and one from Pink the day we left Griffin, yours written the 11th and hers the 12th. They were perused with much pleasure. I was proud to hear from you all and know that you were all well. I would like very much to see you all but don't know when I will have that pleasure now. But I still hope and pray for better times. You must pray for me that I may lead a life of usefulness to be returned safely to you again. Tell the Negroes all howdy for me. Give my love to all friends and relatives and write to me soon and give me all the news. I will have to close and go out camp. We will go to the same camping ground. Receive my best love and wishes for you and children. Yours,

William Dickey 67

Captain Morgan, Company E of the 7th Regiment, Georgia Militia, was with his men in the fortifications of East Macon as the Alabama cavalrymen swung out through a gap in the defenses. The Southern cavalrymen would be riding into a misty fog to search out the Union army. Wilkinson County boys of Company D of the 8th Regiment and Company H of the 2nd Regiment watched the Southern cavalry move off up the road into the drifting fog, then out of sight, north toward Clinton, Georgia.[68]

The Redding brothers, Privates William and James, dirty and tired, peered into the fog in the general direction the cavalry had ridden. Captain Robert H. Barron went down along the line checking his Company of Jones County troops. With the noise of citizens clamoring to leave Macon behind them and Sherman's army, only God knew how far in their front, there most have been apprehension among the Georgia troops manning the cities defenses.

The dense fog that morning didn't help the defenders as they looked from the city in the general direction the enemy was suppose to be to be coming from. At 10:30 a.m. all telegraphic communication from Milledgeville, Georgias' capitol, to Macon was cut by Union troops. Macon was now completely in the dark about what was happening to their east. Maj. Gen. Henry C. Wayne would report from Milledgeville that, "On Sunday morning, the 20th, my telegraphic communication with Macon was cut at Griswoldville by the enemy..."[69]

One of the militiamen manning the defenses of Macon that morning and trying to slow the Union advance, was Erasmus H. Jordon from near Monticello, Georgia. He wouldn't find out until later, that the Union troops had reached his parents home on that day. Alarmed by reports of Yankees in town, his parents had turned out their stock the previous night. Unfortunately, the cattle and horses wandered back as the Federals arrived. They stole the animals and ransacked the family home. The soldiers "played a chord or two on Mother's rosewood piano in the parlor," wrote Jordan's Aunt Rebecca, "and then poured molasses on it, cut a feather bed open and poured feathers over the molasses." The hogs were then shot, and then the foragers loaded up their loot on horses and, "rode off down the road; each man barely visible on account of the plunder."[70]

On the morning of November 20, private Upton and his fellow 100th Indiana Infantrymen were up eating breakfast early. They would be moving out at 7 a.m., right after eating. On the march they passed to the right of Hillsborough in Jasper county and Tranquilla in Jones county. They marched around 14 miles that day. The 100th Indiana Regiment made camp near Clinton, the county seat of Jones County. To keep warm during the cold Georgia night the Indiana infantrymen tore up and burned some rail fences.[71]

Rice Bull a soldier in the 123rd New York Volunteer Infantry Regiment would write in his diary; "On Sunday, the 20th, we made a good march; the day was pleasant but threatened rain. We were on the main road leading to Milledgeville by way of Eatonton."[72]

The Confederate cavalry was also up early and on the road looking for Sherman's force. On their ride to Clinton they had gotten about ten miles northeast of the city when General Wheeler's Alabama cavalry, under Colonel Hagan, were menaced by small parties of Union cavalry screening for the main Union army. Because of the dense fog that morning, General Wheeler did not see Maj. Gen. Peter Osterhaus' XVth Corps until his men were among the column outside of Clinton. Six Confederate troopers got to within 20 feet of the General Osterhaus' headquarters and captured his servant before Federal cavalry finally chased them out of town in a sharp fire fight.[73]

A brigade of Southern cavalry then threw up a roadblock about four miles outside of Clinton, dismounted and manned it. Colonel Van Buskirk's 92nd Illinois mounted infantry volunteers, pursued the Confederate cavalry down the road. The Federals spotted the rebels and dismounted part of Van Buskirk's command and proceeded to attack the roadblock. The Southerners at the roadblock re-mounted and charged the Northerner cavalry. A sharp fight broke out before the charging rebels pulled back to re-group and then came on again. The fire

from Colonel Van Buskirk's Union cavalry drove the entire
Southern brigade scattering into a nearby forest, back towards
Macon. Colonel Van Buskirk gloating, would say "The entire
brigade of the enemy cowardly ran off...." In the action in and
around Clinton, Georgia, the 92nd Illinois Cavalry suffered a loss
of 42 to General Wheelers Alabamans' loss of five troopers.74

Colonel Van Buskirks command continued to follow Hagan's
Alabama cavalry another four miles and at Walnut Creek which
was only two miles from Macon. Here they again found the
Southern cavalry dismounted and strung out on the opposite side
of the creek. The Confederate cavalry had a battery supporting
their position this time and at 3:30 p.m., Colonel Van Buskirk
brought his artillery up, dismounted his cavalry, and preceded to
open fire. The 10th Ohio, that had been held in the Union
reserve, was ordered to mount and to cross the creek by fours and
take the Southern battery. As they charged across the creek,
fierce fighting ensued with the Ohio cavalry gaining and
capturing the Southern battery for a short time. Before the Ohio
boys could bring the rebel artillery back across the creek the
Confederates regrouped and forced the Federals to retire back to
the other side of the stream. The Southern cavalrymen decided it
was time to get their artillery to safety. They limbered up their
battery and pulled it back towards Macon. At Walnut Creek the
Southerners had inflicted 45 casualties on the Union cavalry of
Colonel Van Buskirk's and reported a loss of only three
Alabamians' in the sharp action. Both sides continued to
underestimate their own casualties in these small skirmishes75

Colonel Van Buskirk then dispatched the 9th Ohio cavalry,
with portions of the of the 5th Ohio and the 10th Ohio, to tear up
a two mile section of railroad tracks and telegraph wire in the
area. In the forenoon he brought in a Captain Ladd, 9th
Michigan volunteer cavalryman. Captain Ladd was to handpick
100 men of the 9th Michigan for a mission into a local town.
They would be sent to Griswoldville with orders to burn public
buildings and destroy the railroad and telegraph lines. Captain
Ladd picked his men, four of whom were Pvt. Joseph Rivett of
Company D and Cpls. A. D. Lawrence and B. C. Bowen as well

as Pvt. James Miller of Company B. The detachment from the
9th Michigan proceeded to mount up and move off toward
Griswoldville about ten miles destination.[76]

Confederate Lt. John Baker, Company H of the 8th Regiment,
Georgia Militia, was with his men manning the trenches
defending Macon when firing broke out. Pvts. William Jolly and
Wiley Vinson and the rest of Company H anxiously peered from
behind their trenches in the direction of the firing. The fog had
lifted by now and the Georgians could make out General
Wheeler's cavalry clashing with General Kilpatrick's troopers
outside of their East Macon defense lines. The Southern cavalry
was being steadily driven back into their fortifications. Finally
the Alabama Cavalrymen came dashing back into the Georgia
troops defenses.[77]

General Gustavus Smith would write,

> I withdrew to Macon, in time to assist in
> repelling a formidable demonstration against
> East Macon, in which the Federals succeeded in
> forcing General Wheeler, with a portion of his
> command, to the bank of the Ocmulgee, in rear
> of our fortifications. During the night Wheeler
> extricated his forces, and passed out to the south
> and east, thus again placing his cavalry on the
> flank and in front of Sherman.[78]

It didn't take long for the rest of General Kilpatrick's cavalry
to catch up with the advance party that was pushing General
Wheeler's cavalry into the Macon defensive lines. At 3:30 p.m.
a line of Confederate militia skirmishers were sent out from the
lines and pushed across Walnut Creek. The Georgia troops
stayed in that position for only a short time, in advance of the
trenches, before returning back to their main lines.[79]

General Judson Kilpatrick arrived on the scene to personally
lead a saber charge on the confederate line at Macon. The Union
cavalry with slashing sabers crashed into the Southern
entrenchments. The Georgians immediately gave way after only

a short fight. The Federals later said they left in a "stampeded and panic stricken" rout at their approach. The Northern cavalry welding their sabers, forced their way into the earthworks and briefly occupied a two-gun battery. But unlike Lovejoy Station, the Georgians only fell back to a second line of defense, making sure this time to bring their weapons with them. Here their officers rallied them and they reformed. The backbones of the boys and old men from Jones, Wilkinson, Montgomery, Monroe, Twiggs and the other Georgia counties stiffened as they deployed and advanced. They resolutely pushed back into the outer defenses that had been occupied by General Kilpatrick's Union cavalrymen. With crackling musket fire and bayonets bared the Georgians surged forward into the outer defenses. This time, unlike Lovejoy Station, the outcome would be different. The Georgia infantry proved too much for the Union troops as they drove General Kilpatrick's veteran cavalry back in such haste, they had to leave seven wounded men on the field. Union cavalry Capt. J. H. Hafford, who had been leading the Federal charge and was the first man into the Confederate line, was trapped beneath his dead horse and was unceremoniously captured by the Georgians.[80]

General Judson Kilpatrick's troopers also left twelve dead horses behind on the battlefield before finally retreating near sundown from in front of Macon. General Kilpatrick was content to just tear up the railroad and telegraph wires for two miles along the river before retiring. The 92nd Illinois Cavalry was left behind to cover his rear as he withdrew from Macon. According to one Southern witness, "a Yankee had run off and left his foot and a leg in a boot" beside Walnut Creek. This battle could only have bolstered the Georgia troops' morale. They had stood their ground against veteran Union cavalrymen led by commander Gen. Judson Kilpatrick and had driven them off. Later there would be reports of misconduct by some of the Southern troops after this skirmish at the defenses of Macon.[81]

Felix Pryor, 2nd Brigade, Georgia Militia, wrote his wife of the trying days he had just experienced,

Dear Nancy:

I drop you a few lines to inform you how and where I am at this time. I am in tolerable health at present but am fatigued and tired from recent marches and exposure,&c. We left Lovejoy last week and arrived at Macon Friday, marching 50 miles distance and rode our cars from Forsythe to Macon about 25 miles. We were very tired and worn out when we arrived here. On Sunday evening the enemy made an attack on some of our forces near the est side of this town, and on Sunday night the militia were marched through the rain and mud to this point, where the attack had been made, (Defenses of Macon), expecting to be in a fight early on Monday morning. But the enemy had withdrawn and left....82

The *Chronicle and Sentinel* newspaper would give an account of the battle at East Macon,

On Sunday, November 20th, just at three o'clock P.M. the enemy made an attack on East-Macon at the same place where Stoneman and his raiders made their attack. It was principally an artillery battle, but small arms were also used. The enemy's shells fell in the yard of the workshops of the Central Railroad, but did no injury, and no one was hurt by it. The cannonading was quite active and lasted some two hours. During the time the enemy captured one of our batteries, but it was soon re-captured by our troops and a number of prisoners taken.

About dark our forces succeeded in driving the enemy back, pursuing them about a mile and a half. They left their dead and wounded on the field. Their force we have not ascertained. They were dispersed and driven in the direction of

Griswoldville. They appeared to be tired and
frightened and many of them left their ranks and
wandered off beyond the range of our guns.
They tore up about three miles of the road
beyond Walnut Creek bridge, but it was soon
repaired. While the engagement was going on,
the employees of the Central Railroad removed
all the engines and cars from East Macon and ran
them into the city.

Some of our troops behaved badly in East
Macon by plundering and committing other
depredations after the enemy were driven off.
We forbear to give details.83

While General Kilpatrick threatened Macon, the Confederates
had concentrated what meager forces they had on that city far
from where General Sherman's front was now located. The feint
had worked to the North's benefit. Confederate General Smith
and General Wheeler both accepted credit for having saved
Griffin, Forsyth, and now Macon. Perhaps rightfully so, for if
General Kilpatrick's cavalry hadn't run into General Wheeler's
cavalry or the Georgia troops manning the Macon defenses, what
would have stopped him from riding in and burning and sacking
the city? Kilpatrick was already on the outskirts of East Macon
within a mile or so from the city. It would have only taken an
hour or two out of their line of march to capture Macon. The city
of Macon would have been a prize worth destroying for the
Union army. It would have been a feather in General Sherman's
cap.84

During the war Macon manufactured small weapons, cannon
and shot for the Confederacy. The South was in the process of
building an ammunition laboratory on the Macon and Western
Railroad at Vineville. Located at the Tattnall Square section near
the South-Western Railroad was the armory. The armory's
buildings covered some 10 acres and the main building was 900
feet long. Small arms were made in this building which James
H. Burton had built. Located between the armory and the river

was the big foundry which Robert Findlay had established some years before the war. The foundry turned out "Napoleons" for the Confederacy. A short distance from the foundry there was a pistol and sidearm factory. Nearby, even City Hall had been put to military use as a hospital since the Battle of Chickamauga. On Mulberry Street a percussion cap factory produced its goods. On Cherry and Fourth Streets, W. J. McElroy had turned his tin shop into a sword factory. Women in a factory located near Fifth Street turned out cartridges. Besides the munitions works in Macon, the city also held some 20,000 sacks of corn in three large warehouses located near the depot. Another prize for the raiding Union cavalry could have been the $1.5 million in Confederate gold kept in Macon for the Southern treasury.[85, 86]

But General Sherman wasn't searching out Confederate troops to destroy. His main objectives on this march was to capture Savannah and on the way there, to destroy the Southern capacity and the will to fight this war any longer. He also wanted to break the Southern morale. He did not want to delay his army in seeking out enemy forces. His main concern during the march was to seek out food and forage to sustain his army. Although he was confidant there were no Confederate armies between his army and the sea, he was worried his force could bog down at every city or town. Likewise, if they searched out combat units throughout Georgia, it would drastically delay and could eventually threaten his army. If the enemy attacked, General Sherman would fight, otherwise his army would move to the Sea.[87]

General Sherman's army was like water seeking its own level. When it ran up against something, such as the defenses in Macon, they flowed around and continued on to the sea. Macon wasn't one of their main objectives. If the Southern leaders gave him no opposition, wouldn't this be an invitation to take Macon? General Kilpatrick's cavalry would certainly have been in a position to oblige them. General Smith's Georgia infantrymen and General Wheeler's cavalry didn't give them the invitation. Macon was sparred the pillaging and burning from the Northern army. Other cities and towns in Georgia weren't as lucky.

Flames marked General Sherman's path along the Ocmulgee River. Union Gen. O. O. Howard had arrived in Hillsboro on November 20, 1864. A Georgia woman, Louise Caroline Reese Cornwell would never forget it. She wrote that, "while Gen. Howard sat at the table and asked God's blessing, the sky was red from flames of burning houses."[88]

At the end of the day Private Jesse Dozer, 26th Illinois would write, "November 20th 1864 Sunday very cloudy & rainy We started before the troops before daylight. We went through Hillsboro and marched until 8 o'clock in the evening through mud & water. Forage was plenty."[89]

Sunday night November 20, 1864, with the temperature hovering in the low 50's, General Wheeler's men could get no rest as again they moved out of Macon to harass the Federal advance. Fearing General Wheeler's active cavalry troopers, the Federals transferred their trains to the inside track of the march being taken by the XVIIth Corps to the east. Union troops camped close together for support, but the swarming tactics being used by the Southern troopers persisted in interrupting their rest at night.[90]

The Georgia troops manning the defenses of Macon, could only hope that their continuous movements would not bring them into direct contact with the main body of Sherman's army. Their movement's from Lovejoy through Hampton, Forsyth, Griffin and then to Macon, had so far only brought them into skirmishes with units of Kilpatrick's cavalry. They could only be asking themselves, where was the Union infantry? So far the Union calvary had done an excellent job of screening for the main Federal force. The Southern troops had to be thinking that sooner or later the two forces would collide, but where and more importantly when? Wheeler's cavalry, exiting Macon, hoped to bring back answers to these questions.

7   Thin Gray Line

A thin gray line was all that stood between General Sherman's army in central Georgia and ultimately Savannah. This thin gray line was composed of General Gustavus Smith's 3,700 Georgia Militia and General Wheeler's cavalry of about the same number. They were the South's last and only line of defense against the invading Northern army. To the Union army, it seemed many more were harassing their march. It felt as though everywhere the Union cavalry went, General Wheeler's force was there or wasn't far behind, ready to sting and withdraw. The Southern cavalry was constantly hitting the Federal supply columns, stragglers and foragers. Any blue uniform outside of the main column was at risk of being captured by Southern cavalry, or worse, hung from a walnut tree.

General Wheeler had to do as much damage to the Union army as he could without endangering his own command. Wheeler's command was the only cavalry force shadowing the large Northern army. On the bitter cold morning of November 21, General Wheeler's horsemen were on the move again. His cavalrymen galloped from the Southern lines in pursuit of the Federal cavalry who had encamped the previous night on the road and railroad leading from Macon to Milledgeville. Six miles east of Macon, three regiments of Confederate cavalry charged the barricades of the 92nd Illinois Mounted Infantry and were driven back at a cost of 65 dead and wounded.[1]

At 8 o'clock in the morning, Monday, November 21, 1864, the mercury stood in the thermometer at 54 degrees in central Georgia.[2]

Private Dozer, 26th Illinois Infantry, entered this in his diary, "November 21st Monday. Steady rain and very muddy. All of us that were mounted went in front for forage...The Regiment was detailed for train guard...We camped with the rest of the

Brigade. The rebels maid(made) an unsuccessful attack on our train in (pm?)"[3]

Major Hitchcock of General Sherman's staff would write that the road conditions delayed the march until 11:00 am for some units. The men "floundered through heavy clay mud, which had the consistency of wax or molasses."[4]

Early in the day Capt. Frederick S. Ladd, 9th Michigan Cavalry, took his 100 handpicked men toward the small Georgia town of Griswoldville. From Clinton, where the 9th Michigan was encamped, all the way to Griswoldville, the Southern cavalry had been picketing the roads. Trying to avoid them, Captain Ladd took his men through the Georgia pine woods. It took much longer, but it was safer. Reaching Griswoldville, he lined his 100 men up among some pines to charge.[5]

Griswoldville was a small bustling crossroads town in Jones county, central Georgia, on the road from Macon to Gordon. More importantly the Central of Georgia Railroad passed through the town. The railroad had been completed in the late 1840's. Mr. Samuel Griswold of Burlington, Connecticut, moved to Georgia and eventually purchased five thousand acres there in 1839 from the Duncan family. The new town would be named after the Yankee businessman from Connecticut. His estate would include a Mammoth gin works, candle, soap, and furniture factories. Also a grist and saw mill, a brick plant, watch shop, laundry, barns, outhouses, servants and slave quarters. He built 50 to 60 small sized homes for his workers to live in. An undenominational church was also built for the town.[6]

Griswoldville had a population of around 500 citizens and about 100 slaves. Mr. Griswold owned the slaves and was reported to be a good master. He had become one of the richest men in Georgia by the 1860's. Mr. Griswold kept his fortune in two large iron safes, one in the Post Office and the other in his private sitting room at his home.[7]

When the war started, Griswold leased his cotton gin plant to the Confederate Government for manufacturing of Army Colt type revolvers. With the railroad connections and the plant deep in Southern territory, Griswold turned out 100 guns a month.

They produced more revolvers than all the other Confederate revolver makers put together. The six-shot Colt Navy Repeater, was a .36 caliber pistol. The early models had a round barrel housing and the later models part octagon barrel frame. The revolvers would later be known to gun collectors as the "brass-frame Confederate Colt." By 1864 the factory had turned out over 3,500 of the excellent weapons to be used against the North. They were considered by many as the best army revolvers made.[8]

Earlier in the war Governor Joe Brown felt the need for the production of a weapon known as the Pike. It was an eighteen-inch, two-edged blade fastened on the end of a six-foot staff. It weighed about three pounds. In answer to his call, the machine shops in Georgia turned out over 12,000 pikes in the short period they were being made. Samuel Griswold began turning out pikes in Griswoldville bearing his mark *S. Griswold*, until June 1862, when he switched production to making revolvers.[9]

One Southern unit the 30th Regular Georgia Volunteer Infantry had been stationed at a Camp Griswold, located just west of Griswoldville, early in the war. The 30th Georgia had been issued their uniforms at Camp Griswold in 1862. President Jefferson Davis was reported to have passed through Griswoldville on his way to visit the Army of Tennessee earlier in the year[10]

Some of the residents of Griswoldville included Mr. Ichabod Balcom, a hat maker who lived near the church. Nearby Mr. Aaron Stripling lived and sold handmade shoes of leather, with the soles put together with wooden pegs. He also had bloodhounds that he raised and kept. When a prisoner or slave ran away he was summoned to retrieve them, for which he received twenty-five dollars. Mr. Billy James made tubs and baskets. Mr. Bobby Henderson made chairs and Miles Kelly made and sold grain cradles and repaired watches and razors. Most of Griswoldvilles residents had already left before the arrival of General Sherman's army.

Union Captain Frederick Ladd surveyed the town in front of him, looking at over one hundred carloads and seventeen locomotives still sitting on the side tracks near the Griswoldville station. He saw civilians moving about and some Southern cavalry pickets located in the town and beyond on the roads. He turned to his men and gave the order to charge. Corporals Bowen and Lawrence of Company B and the rest of the detachment from the 9th Michigan came hollering and firing from among the pines into the small Georgia town. The Southern cavalrymen, members of the Alabama brigade, apparently caught by surprise, made a hasty exit. They didn't retreat too far, pulling back only to the pine trees close to the village. Here they were within rifle shot of the Union cavalry and they began to keep up a continuing sniper fire at Captain Ladd's men as they went about their business.11

Captain Ladd ordered his men to destroy the locomotives and burn the cars. They also destroyed a water tank, twenty tons of iron and four hundred boxes of soap. One of his men from company D, private Joseph Rivett took a ball to the hip from one of the Confederate snipers peppering them from the tree line. The Michigan troopers continued to fire back at the Southern cavalrymen while they went about their work of ripping up the heavy train rails of the Central and Georgia Railroad. They would brake and bend the rails around the trees. More importantly they located and destroyed the Griswold pistol factory. Captain Ladd and his men were thorough, some of the tracks were found later some 50 yards from the train tracks.12

Captain Ladd's men of the 9th Michigan Cavalry began burning the public buildings and the train station in retaliation for the continual sniping from the Southern horsemen. As they were preparing to leave, some of the Michigan troopers brought in one of the Alabama snipers that they had captured. After finishing his task in Griswoldville, Captain Ladd then forced the Southern prisoner to become their guide and lead his little party through the greasy smoke and out of town. The detachment from the 9th Michigan would take a route that they hoped would avoid the Southern snipers and the roads that the enemy would be picketing. His men charged out of the burning inferno of Griswoldville taking their wounded Michigan trooper, Pvt. Joseph Rivett with them.13

Corporals Bowen and Lawrence, along with Private James Miller, all of Company B of the 9th Michigan Cavalry, with all the smoke and confusion, had gotten cut off from the main detachment. Late in returning to Captain Ladd's exiting troopers, they were captured by the Alabama cavalrymen who had come wheeling back into Griswoldville. The three men from Michigan wouldn't finish the "March to the Sea" with General Sherman. It took Captain Ladd and his detachment from the 9th Michigan the rest of the day to rejoin their main unit. The Michigan men had lost three captured and one wounded at Griswoldville and they had left that town a smoking ruin.[14]

New Yorker, Rice Bull serving in the 123 New York Infantry, would write of this day and its weather in his diary,

> The next day (November 21, 1864) we had a severe rain, the first since we left Atlanta. The storm made the road slippery and soft and our trains were delayed so it was late at night when we were all in and the trains were parked. During the day we passed through Eatonton,...that night it cleared and became cold.[15]

On hearing of the destruction of the factories at Griswoldville, General Kilpatrick reported that, "The pistol factory at Griswold that we destroyed was very large and valuable."[16]

On the evening of November 21, the cold Georgia rains came down in torrents. It turned middle Georgia's' roads into muddy sloughs as the temperature turned colder. The lengthy ammunition, supply and pontoon trains had been dangerously slowed down and separated during the strung out Union advance. General Howard, commanding the right wing, feared General Wheeler's cavalry might "cut them asunder" before they could temporarily concentrate again at Gordon, a rail junction located southwest of Milledgeville.[17]

"The citizens say that the Yankees brought cold weather with them." A Union soldier remembered, "it is much colder than they usually have." It would get worse in the night as an uncharacteristic snowstorm hit middle Georgia.18

To better protect the supply trains, Gen. O. O. Howard issued orders, moving two of his divisions towards Griswoldville and the Central of Georgia Railroad. When they arrived, they were about 12 miles from Macon and they preceded to make camp for the night. Howard's orders also commanded one of the brigades from the First Division, XV Corps, to make a demonstration toward Macon and to again try and divert rebel troopers from molesting the creeping union trains, or if necessary, to repel a rumored sortie coming from that direction. General Kilpatrick's cavalry was to assist the infantry with screening of the armies movements.19

The 5th Kentucky Cavalry, Colonel Baldwin commanding, from Col. Eli Murray's 1st Brigade, was on the move early that morning. The day before they had moved within two miles of Macon destroying railroad tracks and moving as the rear-guard of the 1st Brigade, 1st Division. On leaving the railroad they eventually camped five miles from Macon on the road to Milledgeville. The men were still tired in the morning, but after a quick breakfast, they mounted up and moved off down the Central of Georgia Railroad, part of the same railroad they had helped rip up the day before. They followed this railroad into Griswoldville, where some of the buildings were still burning and smouldering from the fires set the day before by Captain Ladd's detachment.20

Colonel Baldwin decided to finish where Captain Ladd's men had left off. He ordered his men to burn the rest of the town. Some would later say the order for the burning of the private dwellings in Griswoldville was again in retaliation for the continual sniping of his troopers by General Wheeler's cavalry who was firing from the pine woods near the town. For whatever reason, the order to burn was given and the remainder of Griswoldville went up in flames, despite the continuing rains that fell.21

The *Macon Telegraph and Confederate* newspaper would report some four days later,

> Every house in Griswoldville was burned to the
> ground except Mr. Griswold's house, the
> residence occupied by a Colonel Grier, a few
> Negro slave houses, bordering on the branch and
> a small frame building occupied by one of the
> operatives of the mill.[22]

The church was fired by the Union cavalrymen as well as
workers homes, barns, soap factory, candle factory and others.
They were all burned to the ground. When Colonel Baldwin's
Federal force was finishing up the torching of Griswoldville,
General Wheeler's Alabama Cavalrymen who had been sniping,
were now reinforced and came on in a charge. They attacked the
barricade the Union cavalry had erected to protect them from the
harassing sniper fire from the woods. Union accounts of the
action claim a loss to General Wheeler's force of some 65 men
killed and wounded. General Wheeler's accounts differ,
claiming a lose to his force of only six and inflicting 36 on the
Federal cavalry. After the brief fighting, Colonel Baldwin's 5th
Kentucky along with the remaining 1st Brigade of the 3rd
Division moved about three miles from Griswoldville before
encamping on the Georgia Central Railroad. Upon reaching
camp Colonel Baldwin sent a detachment out to destroy a quarter
mile more of the railroad.[23]

On the morning of November 21, General Hardee, who had
been appointed temporary commander in Georgia, had only
14,680 men present for duty. The report of the amount of troops
available was dated as of November 20, 1864. The majority of
these troops were scattered along the Georgia coast. General
Hardee no longer felt Macon was the intended target of General
Sherman's army. He now realized it had been a feint and that
General Sherman's march would take him to Augusta where a
large arsenal, foundry and work shops were located. This now
seemed to be the real Union objective. Hardee immediately sent
the 1st Brigade of the Georgia Militia (Carswell's) now
commanded by Georgian Col. James N. Willis, to proceed as
rapidly as possible along the Georgia Central Railroad to

Augusta. In the morning Maj. Ferdinand W. Cook was ordered to get his men ready and follow with the Athens and Augusta Local Defense Battalions. General G. W. Smith was ordered to ready his troops and likewise move on to Augusta with the 2nd, 3rd and 4th Brigades of the Georgia Militia. Captain Ruel Anderson's battery, just that day reassigned to General Smith's Georgia militia, would follow along with his four-gun battery. The two regiments of the Georgia State Line under Lt. Col. Beverly D. Evans would also leave for Augusta under the command of General Phillips.24

General Hardee hoped the Federal troops had already swept east. If they had, the militia could advance unopposed directly on to Augusta. If the enemy were encountered, General Smith's men were to avoid battle and return to East Macon, or if necessary follow General Wheeler's cavalry towards the South. General Hardee himself would soon leave Macon after issuing these orders and within hours of his departure, General Taylor would assume command.25

After issuing the orders, General Hardee left by train and a much safer route around the enemy than his troops were taking on their way to Augusta. General Hardee's trip took him first to Savannah to see about that city's defenses.26

General Smith would later write, "...Whilst on the field in East Macon, he (Hardee) ordered one of the militia brigades to start at once to Augusta, and a few hours later he ordered me to move, next morning, with the remainder of my command and proceed to the same place. A few hours after I was ordered to move to Augusta, General Hardee started to Savannah..."27

Colonel James N. Willis' 1st Brigade, Georgia Militia, moving out a day earlier then the other militia brigades, was lucky enough to slip through the ever tightening Union noose across middle Georgia. The 1st Brigade made slow time on the rutted Georgia red clay roads, but swift enough to unknowingly slip between the Union divisions moving from Atlanta, themselves struggling along on the clay roads. The rains would also fall later in the evening and continue to fall into the night as Colonel Willis's, 1st Brigade, trudged on toward Augusta, not knowing what was to befall their friends, relatives and fellow Georgians in the remainder of the militia.28

General Frank Walcutt, a slender young brigadier from Ohio was given the job of protecting the army's far right flank. General Walcutt, like the men in his brigade, was a veteran of many campaigns. He had fought at the Battle of Shiloh where he was wounded. He had served in the advance on Corinth, Mississippi and then the siege of Vicksburg. He also took part in the recapture of Jackson. He had fought through the Chattanooga and Atlanta campaigns and shortly before the fall of Atlanta he was named a brigadier general. His 2nd Brigade was part of General Wood's division. The 2nd Brigade was made up of the 97th Indiana Infantry Regiment commanded by Col. Robert Catterson, 103rd Illinois Infantry Regiment, 6th Iowa Infantry Regiment, 40th Illinois Infantry Regiment, 100th Indiana Infantry Regiment, and the 46th Ohio Infantry Regiment. The 1st Michigan Artillery, Battery B that was attached to General Walcutt's brigade, consisting of 2-three inch Rodmans, had encamped for the night. General Walcutt's force totaled more than 1,500 men. As the Union infantrymen prepared their dinner that evening, smoke from Griswoldville, still burning off in the distance, hung in the cold evening air. It had rained heavy during the evening and then changed over to sleet and snow flurries. The Georgia clay that earlier had been wet and slippery, now hardened, as the men kindled fires for their evening meal. They tried to keep warm by burning rail fences and any other wood they could find and throw on the large fires.29

Private Theodore Upson and his 100th Indiana Infantry Regiment, which was part of General Walcutt's First Brigade, of General Wood's Division, had camped for the night along with the rest of the Brigade. Private Upson and a friend of his, the patriarch of the regiment, Pvt. "Uncle" Aaron Wolford, were on picket duty, trying to keep warm, when Private Upson noticed his friend was greatly depressed. It was something unusual for him, Private Upson thought. To his inquiry as to what was troubling him, Private Wolford said, "I do not know, but I feel that I have not long to live and when I am gone, I want you to promise me that you will take charge of my things. Send them to my wife and write her all about me." Private Upson tried to cheer his friend up by telling him, " that they would never have another battle and that he had got along safe so far and likely would till the end. But it was all no use, he felt sure his time was nearly out." Private Upson would make the promise to his friend as they continued guard duty.30

The 9th Michigan Volunteer Cavalry Regiment of the 2nd Brigade had spent the day in line of battle, and remained in position all day in weather that had turned nasty. Captain Ladd and his detachment who were part of the 9th Michigan, and were the first to burn Griswoldville, went on picket four miles from Macon where they remained during the cold Georgia night.31

The weather began turning colder, and a piercing wind started to howl through the Georgia pines. Because of the weather conditions and the muddy roads, General Sherman's army was limited to only about eight miles on that day. The Union army was cold, wet and exhausted that night.32

Colonel Milo Smith commanding the 1st Brigade Infantry, 1st Division, XV Corps, which consisted of the regiments: 76th Ohio Veteran Volunteers, Col. William B. Woods commanding; 27th Missouri Volunteer Infantry, Col. Thomas Curly commanding; consolidated battalions of the 31st and 32nd Missouri, Maj. A.J. Seay commanding; 12th Indiana Volunteer Infantry, Maj. E.D. Baldwin commanding; 26th Iowa Volunteer Infantry, Maj. John Lubbers commanding; 29th Missouri Volunteer Infantry, Lieut. Col. Joseph S. Gage commanding. The latter regiment being mounted and was now on duty at headquarters XV Army Corps. Col. Milo Smith marched his force to the railroad not far from Griswoldville, here they arrived near the end of the day and encamped for the night near General Walcutt's 2nd Brigade.33

A Surgeon, E. P. Burton, in the 7th Regiment, Illinois, 3rd Brigade, 2nd Division, listed this entry in his diary that he kept daily, "November 21, 1864-Monday. Camped near Hillsboro, town was burned. This day I went into one planter's house, found him at home and very frightened. He felt worse to see his property all leaving him."34

The rains had turned the red Georgia clay roads to such a quagmire that General Sherman's army was forced to pull down rail fences and cut down trees to construct corduroy roads to get their wagons through. Many of the wagons had sunk hub deep into the red slime. Cursing teamsters whipped their mules and grunting infantrymen were used to push the wagons out of the mud holes. The Union army had been hard at work all day and by the evening they were tired.[35]

In Griswoldville cavalry fire-fights between Colonel Murray's brigade and the Confederate cavalry, still crackled amid the greasy thick smoke clouds until dusk. After dark the Union's rear guard was finally driven out of the town by General Wheeler's exhausted troopers of General Iverson's Georgia brigade. One Confederate cavalryman would say, "The daily skirmishing...had no more effect than a fly would have on the back of a sea turtle."[36]

Later Colonel Murray's tired cavalry brigade would retire from the town and camp on the east fork of Little Sandy Creek one and a half miles northeast of Griswoldville.[37]

8   Let All Of Them Get Warm By The Fire

On a very cold early dawn of November 22, 1864, Lt. Gen. Richard Taylor arrived in Macon by train during a Georgia snowstorm. Taylor, the son of the late President of the United States, Zachary Taylor, was a veteran of General Robert E. Lee's Army of Northern Virginia. He had come from his far off post in Montgomery, Alabama from orders of General P. G. T. Beauregard, to take command of the forces in Georgia. He was to observe General Sherman's army and to draw up plans to defend Georgia. He would later write of his arrival in Macon, "It was the bitterest weather I remember in this latitude. The ground was frozen and some snow was falling. General Howell Cobb, the local commander, met me at the station and took me to his house, which was also his office."[1, 2]

General Cobb proposed to Taylor an immediate inspection of the Macon defenses. Taylor would write, "We'll ride out and see the defenses. I've been up all night, working on them. The Yankees were only twelve miles away at noon of the preceding day." Taylor replied, "I asked what force he had to defend the place. He stated the number, which was utterly inadequate, and composed of raw conscripts."[3]

Lieutenant General Taylor shook his head and answered,

> There's no need to see the trenches, and I hope you'll stop your workmen and let all of them get warm by the fire-which is where I'm going to stay. Sherman's not coming here. If his advance was twelve miles away at noon yesterday, you'd have seen him last night. He'd have come before you had time to finish the works or move your stores. I had observed a movement of stores in passing the railway

> station, and now expressed the opinion that Macon
> was the safest place in Georgia, and advised Cobb to
> keep his stores. This greatly comforted Cobb, who
> up to that moment held me to be a lunatic. Breakfast
> was suggested, to which I responded with enthusiasm,
> having been on short commons for many hours.[4]

In fact, General Sherman and his main body were now nearing the Georgia capital of Milledgeville and meeting no resistance at all. The only gunfire heard by most Federal troops, near the capital, came from barnyards where animals were being slaughtered to feed the Northern army.[5]

Lieutenant General Taylor realized that Georgia's plight was hopeless, but was unable to communicate this to the distraught and inexperienced General Cobb, who saw his home state being laid waste. General Cobb persisted in his plans to defend Macon to the death against General Sherman's hoards, which he felt would arrive at anytime.[6]

While Cobb and General Taylor enjoyed their breakfast, a messenger brought a dispatch that the enemy had turned away from Macon and was heading eastward. The delighted Cobb praised the general's wisdom and confessed that he knew nothing of military affairs, but was serving merely "from a sense of duty."[7]

The Governor had arrived and was announced at that moment. General Cobb laughed. "This is awkward," he said. "Browns's the only man in Georgia I wont speak to." But when the governor entered with several others, General Cobb conferred with them on the State of emergency. Governor Brown told them he had just escaped from Milledgeville as the Federals entered. "People said that he had brought off his cow and his cabbages, and left the State's property to take care of itself." Arriving with Brown were General Toombs and General Smith. General Toombs was contemptuous of regular army officers. He once said, "the epitaph of the Confederate Army will be Died of West Point." There was a lack of enthusiasm as he conferred with General Smith, who had taught at the military academy before the war.[8]

There was a more obvious strain as Brown and General Toombs confronted Gen. Joe Wheeler, of whom General Toombs had said during General Wheeler's recent cavalry raid into Tennessee, "I hope to God he will never go back to Georgia...His band consumes more than the whole army...and will accelerate the evil day."[9]

It was a miracle these gentlemen could agree on anything, but the council managed to act with dispatch. General Smith, as earlier ordered by General Hardee, was sending forth his 3,700 Georgia militiamen from Macon hoping that it could pass around General Sherman's front to the east and then turn northward to reach Augusta in time to help in the defense of that city. General Wheeler's cavalry was ordered to screen the movement.[10]

Since early morning the two Redding brothers were getting ready with the rest of their unit from Monroe county for the march east. The Georgia troops were expected to move out at 8:00 a.m. The Redding brothers and the rest of the Georgians grabbed a quick breakfast before getting their equipment together.

A little further away Capt. A. A. Beall, from Wilkinson county, watched the snow flurries falling from the gray Georgia sky. It was unbelievably cold that morning. The temperature had fallen to 12 degrees overnight and was still below freezing as the troops got moving. Captain Beall turned from the window and told his men to get moving. They were just finishing breakfast. The command came to move out at 8:00 a.m. The men began to stir a little brisker in the cold morning air.[11]

The sixteen year old boy serving in the militia, Pvt. J. .J. Eckles, rolled up his thick home-woven blanket he had used to keep him warm the previous night. He threw it over his shoulder before he joined the rest of his company as they headed to unstack their weapons.

Lieutenant A. T. Smith, Company C of the Augusta Defense Battalion, barked out orders to his men. Lieutenant Poole of the same company assisted him in rousing the men. Privates J. D. Andrews and Jerry Gleason got in line with the others as they made for their rifles and equipment. As they stirred, the men winced at the cold morning air cutting into their faces. The Augusta and Athens Battalions were up before the rest of the command, due to their earlier departure from Macon.

In Colonel Mann's, 5th Regiment Georgia Militia, there were comments about the snow flurries that were falling, as they lined up outside. The Macon boys, thirteen year old Pvt. Bridges Smith and fourteen year old Pvt. W. A. Poe, got in line with the rest of their company. Down the line Pvt. William Caswell, the litter bearer of Company H, made sure he had his equipment. Captain Adams of Company H, walked by checking the men of his company. As they stood in line, some were shivering from the cold wind and the blowing snow. These men from Georgia were unaccustomed to the bitter cold weather.

The 130 men of Anderson's Battery spent a restless night trying to stay warm. Along with the rest of the troops they were up early limbering up their 4-three inch Napoleon guns. Lt. Henry Greaves, from Jones County, got his gun crews up and moving even though they wouldn't be leaving until later in the morning after all the infantry had gotten under way.

Forty-eight year old Sgt. Blanton Nance, Company E, 7th Regiment, Georgia Militia, stood in the cold moving his feet to keep them warm when he heard the order from Captain Morgan of his company to move out. Some of the militiamen were complaining of having to man the trenches and defenses in the bitter cold Georgia night.

The Athens and Augusta Local Defense Battalions under the command of Maj. Ferdinand W. C. Cook were the first to move out some two hours before the other units. They were followed by Lt. Col. Beverly D. Evans' elite Georgia State Line Battalion. After the State Line troops there followed the rest of the militia.12

Overall command of the militia was handed to the senior 'brigadier general present, Brig. Gen. P. J. Phillips. General Smith had been held up in Macon for a couple of hours to procure wagons, munitions, and supplies for his force. He would be absent from his command and miss the ensuing battle. Some historians say the battle would have never been fought had

General Smith advanced with his command. General Phillips was the senior brigadier but also the least experienced in actual combat. He was a longtime militia officer and had spent very little time in the Confederate army. The short stint with the regular army took place in Virginia and ended when he resigned on May 13, 1862, even before Robert E. Lee took over command of what was to be the Army of Northern Virginia. Some of his soldiers would later say General Phillips had been drinking the morning of the 22nd. This could explain some of his actions later in the day at Griswoldville. According to his orders from General Smith, General Phillips' immediate destination was Griswoldville. Upon arriving at Griswoldville, General Phillips was to await further instructions from General Smith who would still be in Macon.13

General Smith complied with Hardee's order and moved the militia early in the morning. It was 8:00 a.m., Tuesday November 22nd, as General Phillips and the rest of the militia along with the State Line troops marched out from East Macon on the Georgia Central Railroad and the Macon-Gordon road which ran parallel to each other. Some 12 miles east was the village of Griswoldville, Georgia. General Phillips and his force was on a head-on collision with the Federal right wing.14

In another part of the city while still having their morning breakfast, General's Cobb, Taylor and Smith along with Governor Brown had decided to withdraw the Georgia troops from the path of Sherman. General Taylor would later write, "I told the Governor that his men would be captured unless they were called back at once; and Smith, who undertook the duty in person...This 'army' had some hours before marched east toward Savannah, taking the direct route along the railway."15

The mercury had dropped 24 degrees in 24 hours. It was the coldest and earliest winter that Georgians could remember. At 8:00 a.m. that morning it read 30 degrees as the militia had marched out of the East Macon fortifications. Time had not been on the side of General Phillip's command. The Georgia troops would be well on their way to Griswoldville when the order to withdraw them from Sherman's path was finally issued.1

9   Avoid a Fight With a Superior Force

Daybreak of November 22, 1864, found what was left of Griswoldville still in the hands of the Confederate cavalry. The Southern cavalry reoccupied the town after the departure of the Union cavalry late on the previous day. Units of General Wheeler's cavalry had inflicted some 36 casualties on the Union cavalry, suffering six losses themselves in the previous days hard fighting in and around the little manufacturing town. It was painfully cold the morning of November 22, with snow flurries falling from the grey skies, as the Confederate cavalry began picketing Griswoldville.[1]

Rice Bull from the 123rd New York Infantry wrote, "On the 22nd Reveille sounded early but we were not to march for some time as ours was the rear division, but everything was hurried that morning...by eight o'clock we were marching."[2]

Union Colonel Oscar Jackson would write in his diary of the cold,

> Very cold this morning, and the ground is
> frozen hard. A little snow is in the air. Our left
> wing occupied Milledgeville, the State Capital
> yesterday without a fight, Governor Brown
> having taken the militia and gone to Macon, as
> they expected us there first.[3]

Captain Frederick Ladd and the 9th Michigan cavalry had breakfast early, packed, mounted and moved east away from Griswoldville. They would make ten miles that day before encamping for the night.[4]

Private Jesse Dozer, 26th Illinois, entered this in his daily diary of the march, "November 22nd 1864 Tuesday Cool & windy the rain over We started with(h) the Division in the morning. It was not to safe to forage we were near Macon. There was heavy skirmishing in our front."[5]

Other Union units were also on the move east, in fact the entire column would be passing near Griswoldville on their move to Savannah. The Union supply trains would need shielding from the roving bands of Confederate cavalry and the militia that was thought to be in Macon.

Early in the morning Brig. Gen. Charles R. Woods, commander of the 1st Division, received an order from General Osterhaus commanding the XV Army Corps. He was ordered to take up a strong defensive position near a church and with one brigade to make a demonstration in the direction of Macon. Again the Union army would make one last feint to Macon to confuse the Southerners before preceding east.[6]

General Wood selected the 2nd Brigade, commanded by Brig. Gen. Charles Walcutt, composed of the following regiments: 40th Illinois, Lt. Col H. W. Hall commanding, 206 enlisted men; 46th Ohio, Lt. Col. I. N. Alexander commanding, 218 enlisted men; 103rd Illinois, Maj. A Willison commanding, 219 enlisted men; 6th Iowa, Maj. W. H. Clune commanding 177 enlisted men; 97th Indiana, Col. R. F. Catterson in command with 366 enlisted men; 100th Indiana with Maj. R. M. Johnson commanding 327 enlisted men. Gen. Walcutt had 1,513 troops present for duty and one battery under the command of Captain Arndt, two guns of Battery B, First Michigan. At 6:00 a. m. General Walcutt got his men moving in the direction of Griswoldville, where shots could be heard.[7]

The 9th Pennsylvania cavalry Regiment under the command of Major Appel had thrown pickets out early in the morning, in the vicinity of Griswoldville, where they met and were attacked by General Wheeler's cavalry of General Iverson's Georgia Brigade. A spirited fight developed in the fields to the northeast of Griswoldville.[8]

Encamped nearby was the 5th Kentucky Cavalry Regiment, Colonel Baldwin commanding, part of Colonel Murry's Brigade. Hearing the shots and shouts of the 9th Pennsylvania as they skirmished with the Confederates, he formed up his regiment for battle. Colonel Baldwin was soon assured by Major Appel of the 9th Pennsylvania, that he had things well in hand and wouldn't need his assistance. Major Appel said his Pennsylvania troopers would hold their position.9

Colonel Baldwin preceded to line his regiment in position of battalions in echelons just incase he was needed. He then put one of his battalions behind barricades for defensive action. He could still hear considerable yelling and firing coming from the 9th Pennsylvania camp. Baldwin decided to ride over and check things out.10

Upon arriving Colonel Baldwin found that indeed Major Appel's troops were handily driving the enemy back toward some woods. An orderly of Major Appel's told Colonel Baldwin that the 9th Pennsylvania had cut off and trapped a group of rebels in the woods on his right. Colonel Baldwin sent an order to Captain Glore of his battalion to attack the woods and either capture or drive the rebels from it's protection.11

Scarcely had Captain Glore's battalion advanced when fugitives from the 9th Pennsylvania came dashing down the road pell mell. Word was immediately brought to Colonel Baldwin that confirmed his suspicion, that Major Appel's command was now being driven from the field. Colonel Baldwin immeadiatly gave the command for Major Cheek's battalion to form across the road for the double purpose of reassuring the men of the 9th Pennsylvania and of charging the enemy should he again cross the ravine in their front. Brigadier General Ferguson's division of cavalry of General Wheeler's command came down the road on either side of Captain Glore's battalion, saw the Union cavalry in formation and withdrew. Captain Glore held his men in line. To charge the enemy would have taken him into a heavy swampy area. Colonel Baldwin held his position until General Walcutt's Union infantry arrived to help support him.12

General Walcutt's men splashed forward through Big Sandy Creek and then a swamp, laughing and cheering as they marched to the relief of the Union cavalry. After wading the creek and swamp they passed through some woods arriving in an open field that was held by Confederate horsemen. General Wheeler was on the field and in personal command of the Southern cavalry as General Walcutt's Brigade burst from the woods. Walcutt's infantry formed in line of battle and proceeded to drive the Southerners back through the open field. A heavy and spirited fight ensued. Major Johnson, 100th Indiana Infantry, would later report of the action, "We soon drove them from this position, and as they retreated the column moved forward, driving the enemy before us some two miles and a half." It developed into "quite a little action," noted a Union participant.[13, 14]

At around 11:00 a.m. Maj. Ferdinand W. C. Cook's command made up of the Athens and the Augusta Battalions were still marching down the Macon-Gordon road which was located beside the railroad. They pulled up one mile short of Griswoldville. The Georgians could hear firing and see smoke rising from the town. The only visible buildings they could make out still standing in Griswoldville, besides the few homes, were large brick smokestacks from the foundry. Major Cook quickly got his men into battle line formation astride the Central of Georgia Railroad tracks. But remembering his orders not to seek engagement with the enemy, Major Cook decided not to advance with his command. In line of battle, Major Cook notified Macon of the situation and waited for further orders.[15]

The firing Maj. Ferdinand Cook's men heard was from Confederate General Ferguson's Cavalry regiment. General Wheeler, realizing that General Sherman's army was moving east, had taken most of his command and left the area earlier in the morning. Wheeler left General Ferguson's regiment to screen the movements of General Phillips' troops. General Wheeler had sent the balk of his force across the path of the Union right wing to impede the left wing of Sherman's army from reaching Augusta.[16]

Major Cook's men were two hours ahead of the rest of the Georgia Militia, who were now moving slowly along the same route the Athens and Augusta troops had traversed earlier from East Macon. Their march slowed by crusts of ice that had formed on the road from the previous day of rain and the freezing weather. As the men marched it crunched and shattered beneath their feet.17

Earlier in the morning Union Gen. Charles Woods, 1st Division commander, ordered two regiments of his command, the 76th Ohio Infantry from Colonel Smiths 1st Brigade and the 9th Iowa Infantry from the all Iowa 3rd Brigade of Col. James Williamson, to work at tearing up the railroad. They proceeded in destroying some four miles of track, in addition to a large trestle-work bridge that was burned by the 76th Ohio.18

With his 76th Ohio Infantry on duty tearing up railroad lines, Col. Milo Smith commander of the 1st Brigade, moved his men out, marching about three miles before halting. Colonel Smith ordered his men into position on each side of the Gordon to Griswoldville road. The men of the 1st Brigade immediately began to put up a line of defensive works.19

In the middle of the area where Col. Milo Smith's men were constructing their fortified line there was the old Mountain Springs Baptist Church. The church was located one mile east of the crossing and had derived its name from an old spring at the bottom of a deep incline. The Baptist church was built in 1838 of logs, with a stick and mud chimney. It was equipped with handmade benches for seats. Colonel Smith's men began to dig trenches through the church yard and cemetery. They also began to tear the building down using the logs in erecting their breastworks. Division headquarters would also be located here with ammunition supplies as well as medical assistance.20

As the men of the Smith's 1st Brigade worked on their fortifications, they could hear the continuing skirmishing about a mile west to their front where General Walcutt's 2nd Brigade was located. Shortly a messenger came in ordering Col. Milo Smith's 1st Brigade to move in support of General Walcutt's troops. Colonel Smith's command advanced only three-quarters of a mile when he was then ordered to return to the works which he had just left. Also he was commanded to extend his entrenchments to the right and left. Colonel Smith about faced his men and marched them back to the church they had just come from..21

Meanwhile General Walcutt's command stood in line of

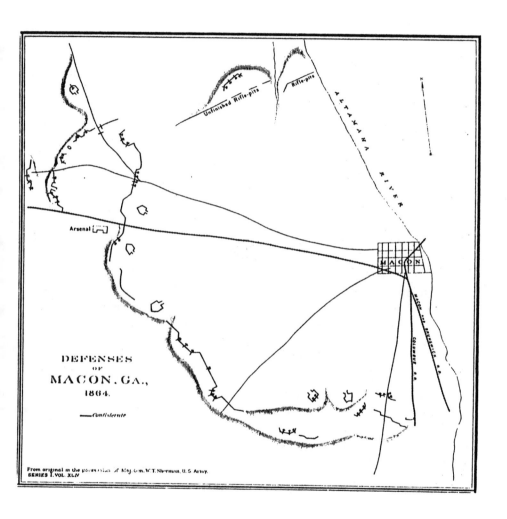

DEFENSES
OF
MACON, GA.,
1864.

——— Confederate

From original in the possession of Maj. Gen. W. T. Sherman, U. S. Army.
SERIES I, VOL. XLIV.

battle with the 5th Kentucky Cavalry and the 9th Pennsylvania Cavalry Regiments, part of Col. Eli Murray's 1st Cavalry Brigade. On that cold morning, they held that line with the infantry until 10:30 a. m. near the Duncan farm.22

Colonel Baldwin then received orders from General Kilpatrick for his 5th Kentucky Cavalry to join him in searching for a Confederate wagon-train that was reported to be passing near them with an attached small infantry guard. The 5th Kentucky rode away from General Walcutt's troops and moved to the left. After riding close to a mile they came in sight of the wagon-train. It had a strong guard of General Wheeler's cavalry, not the expected infantry moving with it on the road. Colonel Baldwin immediately formed his regiment in a open field within full view of General Wheeler's command. The two forces were about four hundred yards from each other as both sides opened fire for a long five minutes. Bullets were flying as Adjutant Mitchell from the 5th Kentucky found himself on the ground. Mitchell's horse had been shot out from under him.23

Colonel Baldwin was relived when he finally received the order to retire from the field. He would later write that, "I most gladly left what I thought a very close place." He had lost three Kentuckians wounded and four horses killed before they pulled back.24

Shortly before this skirmish ended, Federal General Walcutt's 2nd Brigade was on the move marching west two and one half miles down the Griswoldville road in the direction of the latest cavalry fight. He was following the orders given him earlier by Gen. Charles Woods, that his brigade would make a demonstration in the direction of Macon. As his men advanced, they were being passed going in the opposite direction by the 5th Kentucky cavalry being pushed in hard by the Confederate cavalry. General Walcutt immediately sent out his skirmishers from the 46th Ohio and continued to move his command forward toward Griswoldville. The Union skirmishers had only moved about forty paces when they encountered a strong line of Confederate cavalry. The 46th Ohio opened fire as the Confederate cavalry mounted a fierce charge against their line.25

General Charles Walcutt's Brigade immediately was put in line as his skirmishers retreated back to rejoin their brigade's battle line. The Confederate cavalry was allowed to advance to within thirty yards before the order for the infantry to fire was given. With a blaze of muskets several horses went down spilling their Confederate riders on the ground. Under this heavy and galling fire General Wheeler's cavalry hastily withdrew leaving several dead horses and one prisoner on the field. General Walcutt's infantry continued its westward advance.26

The skirmishing between General Walcutts's men and General Wheeler's Confederate cavalry continued back through the smoking Griswoldville. Both sides were taking light casualties as the Federals drove the Southerners west beyond the town. Feeling the object of the reconnaissance having been accomplished, General Walcutt decided to retire the entire brigade one mile back through Griswoldville, towards the east. From Griswoldville, Walcutt's Brigade marched a further mile and a half eastward where they took position on the old Duncan farm. There they were ordered to hold that position until the remaining troops of the column and trains of General Sherman's army passed by, then act as a rear-guard to the entire Union column before they too would follow.27

The cold wind and snow flurries bit into the faces of the Georgia militiamen as they continued on down the Macon-Gordon road and railroad toward Griswoldville. They hadn't heard any firing or seen any Federals since leaving Macon. The hard packed frozen road was now beginning to thaw, making it harder to march on. As the Georgia troops moved along, the red clay began to stick to their feet, adding weight to their bodies. Capt. A. A. Beall and Pvt. Henry Mercer, from Wilkinson County and the rest of the Georgian's, pulled their collars up on their coats to try and keep warm in the cold wind. Their hands and feet were numb from the cold and they were already exhausted from the several days of marching and fighting. The command was strung out over a mile along the road to Griswoldville. General Phillips, on horseback, moved east with his troops on the muddy tracks of the Georgia road.

Private William Caswell, litter bearer of Company H, 5th Regiment, Georgia Militia, like the rest of the Georgia troops with their dirty gray cotton uniforms wet, felt chilled in the wind. Although they had been marching for three hours, they were still about two hours from Griswoldville and maybe some dinner. Several Negroes slaves marched with the Georgians down the road. They served as cooks and orderlies for some of the Confederate soldiers in the militia.

Private W. A. Poe, fourteen years of age, of the 5th Regiment Militia, was now just ten days away from his December 2nd birthday as he marched on the wet red clay road. His hands were numb from the frigid cold. The temperature was slowly warming, but it was still hovering around the freezing mark as the militia plodded along.[28]

About 1:00 p.m. the Redding brothers, Sgt. Blanton Nance and the others in the militia looked ahead though the swirling snow flurries. They could make out troops in battle formation to their front a short distance down the road. The troops were found to be the Athens and Augusta Battalions. The command came to a stop. The men nervously looked to their front where the Athens and Augusta Battalions where drawn up in battle line.[29]

Felix Pryor a member of General Phillip's 4th Brigade now under the command of Colonel Mann would write to his wife on November 23, 1864, "...On yesterday morning we left camp and marched down the road in pursuit and came to where they were in the evening, a mile or two below Griswoldville..."[30]

Brigadier General Pleasant Phillips' men had reached a point one mile east of Griswoldville. General Phillips would write in his report, "The command left East Macon at about 8 a. m. and arrived without incident at 12 or 1 o'clock within about one mile of Griswoldville." There they found the two battalions of Athens and Augusta troops drawn up in a line of battle. The line was facing in the direction of Griswoldville on the Macon-Gordon road and the Central of Georgia Railroad. General Phillips met a number of General Wheeler's cavalrymen belonging to Brig. Gen. Samuel W. Fergusons Division, all of whom informed him that the Federals were in Griswoldville in force, about 800 to a 1,200 strong. They mentioned to General Phillips that they had been skirmishing with them all day long. After conferring with Phillips, this only remaining detachment of General Wheeler's cavalry left in the area rode off to join General Wheeler who was now trying to get in front of General Sherman's moving army. With their departure, Phillips' command was now left without cavalry support.31

General Phillips conferred with his Georgia brigade commanders. His orders specifically stated, first from General Toombs, "...avoid a fight with a superior force." Secondly his Commanding officer, General Smith, "If pressed by a superior force, fall back upon this place without bringing on a serious engagement...." Both mentioned a "superior force." General Phillips' command numbered more than 4,000 including Captain Anderson's Battery. General Wheeler's cavalry informed him of perhaps 800 to 1,200 to his immediate front in Griswoldville. Phillips had odds of three to one against the Union force. His orders also stated that he and his command were to march to Augusta. The route to Augusta went through Griswoldville. He decided his force would proceed in that direction.32

General Pleasant Phillips ordered his Georgians to form a battle line. He put General Anderson's 3rd Brigade on the right, the Athens and Augusta battalions on his immediate left, and Brig. Gen. Henry McCay's 4th Brigade on the far left of the line. He then placed Colonel Mann's 2nd Brigade in the rear as reserves. The 400 men of Lt. Col. Beverly Evans' elite State Line were deployed in a strong skirmish line to the front. They began their advance on Griswoldville still smoking in the distance only one mile away.33

Captain John J. McArthur got his 26 men of Company C in line with the rest of the 7th Regiment, Georgia Militia. Pvt. Groves Connor, Pvt Andrew J. Coursey, Pvt. John W. McArthur and the others from Montgomery County, with muskets in hand, faced toward Griswoldville.34

General Toombs in Macon fired off a dispatch to General Phillips at 12:20 p.m.,

General: Wheeler having retired to the right,
keep a close lookout with your skirmishers and
avoid a fight with a superior force. You can best
judge of the direction. The wagon train will not
leave this evening. P. S.-If it be dangerous to get
back, take down the Marion road.35

Twenty-five minutes later General Smith fired another
dispatch off to General Phillips. He had received Major Cook's
dispatch that had been sent around ll:00 a.m. It had taken around
two hours to communicate between the militia at Griswoldville
and Macon. It's safe to say that General Philips would have
received the 12:20 p.m. dispatch sent from Macon around 1:30-
2:00 p.m. 36

The latest order from General Smith in Macon read,
General:
Since this note was written a courier has
come in from Major Cook stating that the enemy
were advancing upon him at Griswoldville. The
wagon train is still here, and it had already been
determined not to send it by the route you are on
before this information came in. If pressed by a
superior force, fall back upon this place without
bringing on a serious engagement, if you can do
so; if not, fall back upon the road indicated in
General Toombs' note. Captain Anderson's
battery started out this morning. Has probably
joined you. Let me know as soon as possible
exactly what is going on in your front. G. W.
Smith.37

Another note came from Capt. E. Hawkins, Aide-de-Camp to
Smith to General Phillips,

If the brigades are not concentrated before
this reaches you, Captain Hawkins is instructed
to show this to each brigade commander and to

Major Cook. If Captain Anderson's battery has
not already joined the infantry, it will return to
this place or join the infantry, as may be best in
the opinion of the ranking officer present.38

At around 2:00 p.m., General Phillips' command with the 400
men of Lt. Col. Beverly Evans' Georgia State Line thrown out in
front pushed into Griswoldville which was still smouldering from
the fires set the previous day. The boys and men from Augusta,
Athens, Macon and the other cities and counties of Georgia fully
expected to be walking into Union fire. The Southerners kept
their cold fingers on the triggers of their weapons as they moved
among the burned out buildings and ruins that had been
Griswoldville. There were no Union troops in the village, just a
greasy black smoke rising from the ruins which added more
grime to their already dirty gray uniforms. The smoke mixed
with snow flurries as the troops searched through the burned
village.39

General Phillips would later write in his official papers about
Griswoldville, "Where the enemy had just burnt some buildings
and retired before we arrived, of which facts I informed the
major-general commanding at about two o'clock p.m."40

This was the first town the Georgia troops had followed
General Sherman's army through since his march had begun.
The Georgians from Monroe, Wilkinson, Jones and other
counties as well as the troops from the cities of Macon, Athens,
Augusta and towns like Dublin, saw the complete destruction of
this small Georgia town. These Georgia boys and men didn't
like what they were witnessing. Everything had been destroyed,
burned to the ground. Everything, all the rumors they had heard
about General Sherman was true. As they filed through
Griswoldville they thought of their own towns and love ones in
Georgia and their fate if the Federals weren't stopped.

They saw Mr. Griswold's house still standing, but his barn
had just been torched by the Union troops and most of the smoke
in the town was coming from that blaze. They could see another
house down the street that had not been burned and several slave

houses were also unharmed. The rest of Griswoldville was a smouldering ruin.[41]

Sixteen year old Pvt. J.J. Eckles and the rest of the Georgia troops could see the tall smoke stacks made of brick near the foundries still standing in the town. The blackened smokestacks were reaching for the cloudy snowy skies.

Jones County Capt. Robert Barron and the rest of the Georgians searched for the enemy, but none were to be found in the whole town.

Major Ferdinand W. C. Cook and General Phillips conferred on horseback. Major Cook told General Phillips his orders from Hardee were not to engage the enemy and to precede on to Augusta. General Phillips didn't countermand the order and shortly after, Major Cook's command consisting of the Athens and Augusta Battalions marched out of Griswoldville on the Georgia Central Railroad heading east toward Augusta.[42]

Shortly after Major Cook's men left, General Phillips gathered his men and started in the same direction the Augusta and Athens Battalions had gone, down the railroad. He wanted to get his command out of the smoking town then halt and await further orders from General Smith in Macon. The State Line soldiers led the way in a skirmish line along the railroad in the direction of Augusta.[43]

The rear of General Phillips' column hadn't even cleared the village when small-arms fire could be heard crackling some half mile distance in advance of his column. The shooting came from between the advance and rear guards of Major Cook and the enemy. General Phillips ordered his men to advance toward the firing in the direction they were heading.[44]

10   Not Dreaming
of a Fight

After the fight with the Confederate calvary around
Griswoldville, General Charles Walcutt's men had pulled back to
the old Duncan's farm. There is no evidence that Walcutt's force
had spotted Cook's two battalions that had pulled up outside of
Griswoldville before they themselves had withdrawn from that
town. Samuel Griswold had purchased the land the farm was
located on some two decades before and since that time it had
mostly turned to scrub. Upon arriving at the crest, General
Walcutt found the two guns of Capt. Albert Arndt's 1st Michigan
battery already in place. He began positioning his infantry facing
west towards Griswoldville. The 103rd Illinois Regiment took
position to the right of the 6th Iowa Regiment which was in the
center of the line. The 97th Indiana Regiment to the right of the
103rd Illinois Regiment and anchoring the far right was the 12th
Indiana Regiment. The far right of the Union line ended at the
Georgia and Central Railroad and beyond that a lay a swamp.₁

With the 6th Iowa Regiment anchoring the center, the 40th
Illinois Regiment was to their left. Then came the 100th Indiana
Regiment, with the 46th Ohio Regiment anchoring the far left of
the line. The Northerners also had another swamp, the Big Sandy
Creek Swamp located to the left of their line. Arndt's Battery
was situated right behind the Union line, near the center, where
the junction of the 6th Iowa and the 40th Illinois met. The two-
three inch Rodmans straddled a road that led to and from
Griswoldville.₂

General Charles Walcutt's 2nd Brigade had excellent terrain
to defend here on Duncan's farm. The farm site lay below the
railroad two miles southeast of Griswoldville. From the railroad

a wide fallow field gradually sloped to a branch known as the Big Sandy Creek. This small stream meandered through a shallow ravine. Growing about the stream was a thick firing of small trees, gall-bushes, bamboo and swamp growth. The growth stretched about ten yards on both banks. Dry brown cornstalks from the previous growing season still protruded from the Georgia soil in the open farm field to the west of the Union line. From the branch the ground began to rise more steeply forming a ridge. The crest had woods and was located some two hundred yards from the stream at the bottom. There was also a clay packed road that cut across the crest of the hill from Griswoldville. Both roads coming from Griswoldville and leading east to Sherman's Federal wagons were now covered by the Union infantry.3

About 50 yards in front of the Union line, located in the branch just to the right of Captain Arndt's Battery, stood a giant old pine tree. This tree would be a witness to the coming man made storm. It would be an unintended target for hundreds of bullets in the ensuing hours.4

To the rear of where Brigadier General Charles Walcutt had put his men on the ridge there was a woodland that extended for one mile. The line of blue infantry faced west towards Griswoldville and the line ran from the railroad on the right to the Big Sandy Swamp on the left. Duncan's farm house was located in the center of the line, near the junction of the line of the 103rd Illinois and the 6th Iowa and would become a landmark in the impending battle.5

Lt. Colonel Alexander of the 46th Ohio Regiment put his men in line on the far left of the Union line with their left extending to a swamp. The Ohio men would then settle down to their afternoon dinner.6

The 100th Indiana Regiment had followed the brigade to the Duncan farm and was ordered to fill the line to the right of the 46th Ohio. After the Indianans formed their line and had taken up the position assigned them, Major Johnson commanding, directed his men to build slight barricades. Before letting his men get some dinner, Major Johnson had run out some skirmishers in the open field toward Griswoldville. He didn't want any surprises from the enemy, in particular the cavalry they had tangled with earlier in Griswoldville. It was some of these skirmishers that Major Cook's Confederate battalions had just stumbled into just outside of Griswoldville.7

Major Ferdinand Cook watched as his Southern skirmishers forced the ragged line of the enemy pickets down a slope toward the Big Sandy Creek Branch then up a small rise to the opposite crest. On the opposite crest, Major Cook could see the enemy posted in what he thought was a line of battle behind some fortifications.8

Union Lieutenant Charles W. Wills, 103rd Illinois Regiment, would later note in his diary, "November 22, 1864, has been a heyday for our brigade. We were getting dinner, not dreaming of a fight, when a fine line of johnnies pushed out of the woods and started for us."9

The Federals had been on the crest of the hill about one hour when with a rattle of musketry the pickets came crashing back into the Union lines. The Union troops still eating, had to toss their lunch of raw bacon and hardtack into the fires. General Walcutt's 2nd Brigade numbering some 1,513 men began to quickly unstack their weapons and form behind the barricades. Capt. Arndt's Battery consisting of fourteen men began scrambling to service their two-guns.10

They had only been in line less than an hour when Pvt. Theodore Upson and Pvt. "Uncle" Aaron Wolford joined their fellow 100th Indiana Regiment in grabbing their stacked arms. The two good friends stood side by side behind a light barricade and looked down the hill at the Southern skirmish line advancing on them. They saw their own pickets firing and running for the crest and the safety of the Union line.11

Twenty-five of the three hundred and thirty men of the 100th Indiana Regiment were armed with the new repeating Spencer .52 caliber rifles. Those soldiers began loading their new seven-shot repeating rifles. The remaining men of the regiment had the older Springfield rifles .58 caliber muskets. The Indianan's took up their prepared positions which had been erected earlier when they arrived on the hill. Their Commander, Maj. Ruel M. Johnson had made them erect a slight barricade of rails to guard as a precaution against any contingency that might arise. It looked as though that contingency was now arising. His precaution would pay dividends later with the lives of his soldiers hanging in the balance. Other Federal units along the line hadn't prepared any fortifications.[12]

As Major Asias Willison of the 103rd Illinois Regiment, looked across the branch to the Confederates on the opposite rise, he became alarmed that his men had no works for defense. He ordered his men to hastily construct a small temporary line of works. A split rail fence running through the Duncan farm was hurriedly ripped apart by his Illinois troops for their fortification line.[13]

Colonel Robert Catterson would write in his official report, "We had scarcely taken position in the edge of timber skirting the farm on the east when our pickets were fired upon." After his pickets were hurriedly driven into the his line, Colonel Catterson's men of the 97th Indiana Regiment, began scrambling about quickly building a barricade of rails and anything else they could find. Their skirmishers brought news of a large Confederate infantry force immediately to their front. Colonel Catterson's men then lay behind the light barricade "anxiously awaiting his (enemy) appearance." Colonel Catterson estimated the enemy force to his front at between 6,000-7,000 men.[14]

There was concern among the Union force that this Southern infantry force might be working in concert with General Wheeler's cavalry, the same Southern cavalry that they had met earlier in the day at Griswoldville. They continued searching the horizon for the Southern horsemen.[15]

The Union troops on the right-center of the line began tearing several log farm buildings that stood directly to their front, near where Arndt's Battery was located. The logs from the old cabins gave them excellent barricade material and they quickly constructed a makeshift lunette for the guns. What was left of the substructures provided more cover downhill from the main line. Detachments of Union infantry would use these out buildings for breastworks to fire from, some yards to the front of the main Federal line.16

As General Phillips' State Line and Georgia Militia Brigades left Griswoldville along the railroad tracks toward the sound of firing, they had entered a line of pine trees. Here in the safety of the tree line they were halted by their officers. General Phillips then rode in the direction of the firing searching for Major Cook.

General Phillips found Major Cook a short distance from the pines in an open field. When he rode up, Major Cook immeadiatly pointed out the enemy posted on the opposite eminence. It looked to General Phillips that the enemy was in line of battle behind some temporary entrenchments and fortifications. He also noticed that Major Cook's skirmishers were still engaged with the enemy on the left, near the railroad, where the crackling of muskets could be heard. He saw some Union skirmishers scurrying up the hill to their lines, turning and firing as they went.17

General Charles Walcutt ordered his Union infantry to hold their fire until the enemy were well within musket range.18

Cook's skirmishers were well within the range of Arndt's two-gun battery of three-inch Rodmans. As Major Cook's skirmishers on the left near the railroad broke into the open field near an old abandoned depot, Captain Arndt barked out the command to fire. One of the Rodmans fired at the advancing Southern skirmishers. Major Cook's Athens and Augusta skirmishers, surprised by the artillery fire, quickly fell back into the protection of the line of pines. The same pines which had screened the arrival of General Phillips' militia infantry force.19

Under cover of the pines General Phillips again assumed over all command of Major Cook's Athens and Augusta Battalions. From his talk with General Wheeler's cavalry earlier in the day he quickly assumed that this was the force that the Southern cavalry had tangled with. If so, he outnumbered the enemy three to one. Still following his orders from General Hardee, of preceding to Augusta with his command, he began formulating a battle plan to push the enemy aside.20

The Federal artillery, Arndt's Battery ceased firing as the

Northern pickets came scurrying back into their lines. The battlefield grew silent. The Union soldiers stared west across the field wondering when the "rebs" would pull out, not believing that they would advance on their entrenched position.

Union Lt. Charles W. Wills walked among his men of the 103rd Illinois Regiment on the crest, while watching the unfolding scene of the Confederates moving below. He could make out the gray uniforms moving into their alignment among the green background of the Georgia pines.[21]

Privates Theodore Upson and "Uncle" Aaron Wolford, 100th Indiana, waited anxiously with the rest of the regiment behind the rail barricade. They stood side by side with their muskets in hand anxiously watching the Confederates off into the distance.

General Charles Walcutt, with a mustache that flowed into a thick dark beard, walked over to a big pine tree that stood behind where the 106th Illinois and 6th Iowa Regimental lines joined. He stopped and looked across the field again. He, like his soldiers, must have been wondering what the enemy would do next. Union Lt. Charles W. Wills, 103rd Illinois Regiment, would later write of the Northern field of fire, "We had a nice open field without even a fence on it, full 600 yards wide in our front."[22]

Brigadier General Pleasant Phillips' plan of attack called for General Anderson's 3rd Brigade to attack the Federal right flank. Gen. Anderson's entire brigade would be positioned to the left of the railroad. Major Cook's Athens and Augusta Battalions would attack the enemies left flank. Major Cook's men had formed an obtuse angle on the right side of the Confederate line when they aligned in the pines and would have to compensate when they advanced to keep abreast of the rest of the line. General McCay's 4th Brigade of Georgia Militia and Evans' State Line troops would attack the center of the Union line. General Phillips ordered the Georgia troops to charge across the fields to their front into the ravine. Here they were to take shelter in the swampy branch area, 50-100 yards from the Union positions, prior to renewing their assault.[23, 24]

General Phillips then gave the command to form the infantry

lines among the pines. On the far right he placed the Athens
Battalion, to their immediate left the Augusta Battalion, then the
2nd Regiment of Lt. Col. Beverly Evans' State Line, followed
by the 1st Regiment State Line. Then General McCay's 4th
Brigade, to their left and manning the far left of the Georgia line
was General Anderson's 3rd Brigade. General Phillips kept his
own 2nd Brigade, now under the command of Col. James N.
Mann in reserve. In the line of battle they were located behind
General McCays 4th Brigade, near the center of the line.[25]

In Colonel Mann's Brigade, Felix Pryor would later write to
his wife Nancy, "...where we formed a line of battle and marched
up in front of the enemy. Then a fight commenced which lasted
for about three hours."[26]

Capt. Ruel Anderson's Battery unlimbered to the rear of
General Anderson's 3rd Brigade of the Georgia Militia just north
of the railroad in an opening among the pines. Anderson's
Battery would have a good field of fire from their "eligible site"
more than 800 yards distance from the Federal line. A section of
Anderson's Battery, commanded by Jones county native Lt.
Henry Greaves, was placed at the old Number 18 train station.[27]

Captain Anderson's 130 artillerymen began to service their
four Napoleons. The Southern guns were well within the 2,000
yard effective range of the Napoleon field piece. Lt. Henry
Greaves of Jones County, commanding two gun crews, ordered
his men to load shot. The guns were moved into place, men were
busy loading as the horses were led to the rear. The Southern
"Napoleon" guns began to answer the Union fire with a salvo of
their own.[28]

When the Georgians advanced they would have to leave the
cover of the pines for the open field. The field sloped gradually
downward to a small branch of the Big Sandy Creek, a distance
of some 400 yards. They would then go through the cornstalk
stubbled field for another 300 yards to the Big Sandy Creek
Branch. Here there was some cover in the ravine behind the
undergrowth of gall, box berry, reeds, bamboo, briars and small
trees on either side of the stream for about ten yards. Here in the
ravine General Phillips hoped his men could catch their breath

and regroup before they pushed to the top. If they made it to the ravine they would be only 50 yards from the center of the Union entrenchments and because of the bend of the branch 100 yards from the flanks of Union General Walcutt's troops.

Brigadier General Phillips' troops would have to go across 800 yards of mostly open terrain to reach the enemy on the crest of the opposite hill. They would be advancing against entrenched veteran troops, some armed with the new Spencer rifles, and supported by a battery of artillery.[29]

It was about 3:00 p.m. when an Aide-de-Camp to General Smith in Macon, Captain Hawkins, arrived with the 12:45 p.m. note written earlier by Smith. While searching for General Philips the messenger could see the Southern skirmishers coming back into their own lines. Captain Hawkins found Phillips and handed him the message. General Philips read the memo that ordered him not to engage in battle with a larger enemy force. He apparently conveyed his intention, to the Aide-de-Camp, not to attack the Union troops to his front.[30]

Major Cook's earlier dispatch to Macon, reporting the enemy being in the area of Griswoldville in force, had created consternation at headquarters. The movement by the Georgia troops to Augusta had already been postponed by the authorities in Macon. The dispatch from Macon, decided over breakfast, still hadn't been received by General Phillips who was still following his original orders from General Hardee. General Smith's note to Phillips wasn't direct enough. It just ordered him not to attack or engage a force larger than his own. Smith should shoulder a large portion of the blame for the upcoming battle due to his ambiguous order.[31]

Captain Hawkins, the Aide-de-Camp to General Smith, walked away and quickly jotted down a note to his commander who was still in Macon,

> General: The whole division, including Cook's
> battalion, is one mile in advance of this place, on
> the Central railroad, in line of battle, with the
> State Line troops thrown out in front skirmishing

with the enemy. Anderson's battery opened
upon them just as I rode up to the line, the
enemy's battery replying. General Phillips does
not know what their force is, and, on receiving
your instructions, concluded not to advance
further. On the movements of the enemy
depends whether or not he will fall back to this
place or remain where he now is. Captain
Hawkins. P.S. I will remain to see any
developments which may be made before I
report in person.[32]

When General Phillips had first conferred with Captain
Hawkins he must not have been entirely sure of the exact size of
the force in front of him. General Wheeler's cavalry had given
him an earlier figure of 800 to 1,200 Federals in Griswoldville.
However the number of troops behind the mile breastworks on
the opposite rise couldn't be surmised by Phillips. While
Captain Hawkins was away writing, then dispatching his note to
General Smith by courier, the order to move forward had been
given by General Phillips. Phillips apparently had changed his
mind about attacking the smaller Union force situated between
his command and the road to Augusta.[33]
During the same time, fifteen miles away Union troops were
nearing Georgia's capital of Milledgeville. Rice Bull of the
123rd N. Y. Volunteer Infantry would write of the fall of the
Georgia state capitol of Milledgeville event in his diary,

It was cold but fair weather; the roads were
not bad and the nearer we came to the city the
better they were. The country was covered with
plantations and it was a red letter day for our
foragers. By noon the advance was in the
vicinity of Milledgeville and then halted for the
troops in the rear to close up. It was not known
but there might be a defense made of the capital,
as it had been evident there was a small force of

the enemy on our front from Eatonton on toward
Milledgeville. However, it was soon found that
no resistance would be made and by two o'clock
our advance occupied the city.

It was as quiet to all appearance as Madison
had been; all the prominent people had fled. The
Governor of Georgia, the Legislature that had
been in session, the Judges, and all other state
officials had left the capital. Not a hand had
been raised to defend Milledgeville and the
'Yankees' were in possession without firing a
shot.[34]

Militia Brigadier H.K. McCay

Rebel Captain Ruel W. Anderson.

Militia Brigadier General Charles D. Anderson

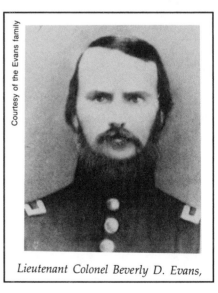

Lieutenant Colonel Beverly D. Evans,

John Bell Hood, CSA—whose northward march would lead to disaster at Franklin, Tennessee.

Joseph Wheeler, CSA

Gustavus W. Smith, CSA

Avid states rights advocate Governor Joseph E. Brown of Georgia. His insistence that state troops only fight on Georgia soil was shared by his general, Gustavus Smith.

Special Collections, University of Georgia Libraries

Brig. Gen. Charles C. Walcutt

Brig. Gen. Orlando M. Poe
Chief of Engineers Sherman's Army

William J. Hardee, CSA

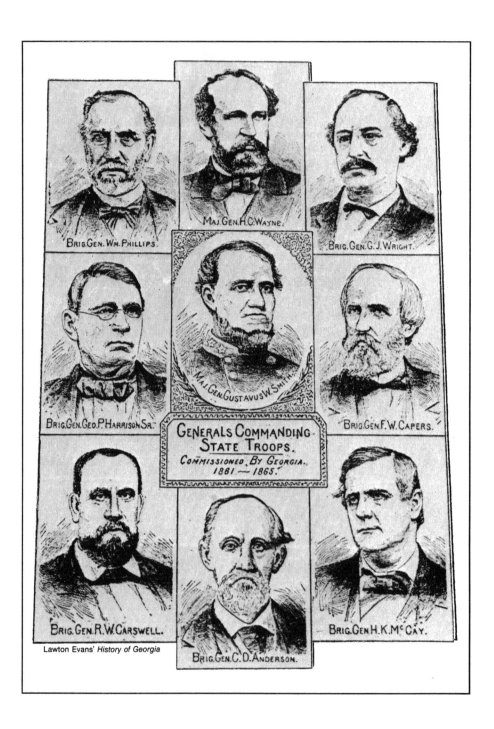

BRIG.GEN. WM. PHILLIPS.

MAJ. GEN. H.C. WAYNE.

BRIG. GEN. G. J. WRIGHT.

BRIG. GEN. GEO. P. HARRISON SR.

MAJ. GEN. GUSTAVUS W. SMITH.

BRIG. GEN. F. W. CAPERS.

GENERALS COMMANDING STATE TROOPS. COMMISSIONED BY GEORGIA. 1861 — 1865.

BRIG. GEN. R. W. CARSWELL.

BRIG. GEN. C. D. ANDERSON.

BRIG. GEN. H. K. McGAY.

Lawton Evans' *History of Georgia*

William T. Sherman, USA

L E F T   W I N G

R I G H T   W I N G

Judson Kilpatrick, USA

Henry W. Slocum, USA

Oliver O. Howard, USA

Jefferson C. Davis, USA   Alpheus S. Williams, USA   Francis P. Blair, USA   Peter J. Osterhaus, USA

Georgia Historical Battle Marker At Griswoldville

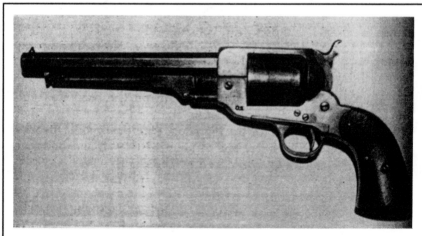

Pistol manufactured at Griswoldville for the Confederacy by Griswold and Grier.
by courtesy of the Confederate Museum at Richmond and Col. Gordon Green.

11 It Was a Terrible Sight

It would take Georgia General, John B. Gordon, to later describe this time of the war and its effect on the soldiers of the Confederacy. Everything had been exhausted by the winter of 1864 and the spring of 1865 except as General Gordon would say, "devotion and valor." The Georgians gathering in the trees near Griswoldville would reach inside for their devotion and valor on this day.1

The Southern officers began hollering out commands as the Georgians started forming into column by brigades among the pines. Some of the men carrying heavier packs dropped them to the ground to lighten their load. Orders to load their muskets were given and attached bayonets for those who had them.

Captain Morgan, Company E, walked among his Georgians. He passed by forty-eight year old Sgt. Blanton Nance, and Pvt. William Warren of his company shuffling in line to keep warm. He checked Privates Erwin, Horton, Johnson, Arthur Newton and the others in his company before turning and facing the far crest to their front where the waiting enemy was entrenched.

Thirteen year old Pvt. Bridges Smith, the young boy from the Macon armament factory, picked up his heavy musket and got in line with the others from the 5th Regiment, Georgia Militia, as the entire brigade dressed in a line.

Fourteen year old Pvt. W. A. Poe, from Macon, also of the 5th Regiment, was probably wondering if he would reach his fifteenth birthday just days away as he stepped in line with his company.

Troops of Company H, 5th Regiment, formed up under the direction of Capt. A. A. Beall. The company litter bearer Pvt. Henry Mercer from Wilkinson County joined the others in line. The 5th Regiment was in the 2nd Brigade under Col. James Mann. The 4th, 5th as well as the 6th Regiments would be held in reserve in the pines with the rest of Colonel Manns 2nd Brigade. The men and boys in Company H were one of two companies, the other was Company D, 2nd Regiment that was formed to serve in the Georgia Militia from the small population of Willkinson County. This county also proudly maintained seven additional companies serving in the field in other Confederate armies.[2]

Colonel Mann and Lieutenant-Colonel Bowdoin rode among the troops of the 2nd Brigade. They passed by Felix Pryor, Seaborn Walker, Poer Fears, George Stovall, Joe Few Jr., stepping in line as the First Division's reserve.

Jones County boys and men were being formed up by their company commander, Capt. Robert H. Barron, in the left of the Southern line. His company was part of Anderson's Brigade, Georgia Militia.[3]

Another part of General Anderson's command was Company H, 8th Regiment, Georgia Militia, also made up of men and boys from Jones County. Lt. John Baker and the other officers of the regiment checked their men as they walked among them. Pvts. William Baker and Wiley Vinson members of Company H, along with the rest of the Georgia troops loaded their weapons with cold numb fingers before forming in line.

Captain John J. McArthur, Company C, 7th Regiment, Anderson's Brigade walked among his remaining 26 men in the cover of the pines. In line among the Montgomery County men were Pvt. William Ryals and Pvt. Uriah Sears.[4]

Hopkins County, Georgia was represented on the line in Anderson's brigade. In line with the 7th Regiment were four soldiers, Pvt. Hiram Gibbs, Pvt. William T. McRae, Pvt. Malcomb McQuaig and Pvt. Henry Nail. They all had been enrolled in the militia in April, 1862.[5]

On the far left of the Southern line, in General Anderson's 9th Regiment, Georgia Militia, the men of Company D were checking their weapons and equipment. Lieutenant Farmer, Lieutenant Swint, 1st Lieutenant Lee and Lieutenant Semms moved among the men getting their alignment formed. In line with this company was a doctor, J. S. Henry. Two Privates John Anderson and Ira Scoggins, in their grimy gray uniforms wet from the snow, positioned themselves in line with the others.6

In the center of the Confederate line the 400 men of the Elite Georgia State Line formed up under their commander, the neatly groomed mustached and bearded, Georgian Col. Beverly Evans. The dark haired, good looking Colonel Evans watched his lines as the ranks filled in, colors to the front.

Private Christopher Biers from the Athens Battalion, Company A color-bearer, his hands numb with cold unfurled the flag and joined his comrades in formation. Private Biers moved to the front with the colors.

On the far right of the line, Company B of the Athens Battalion, the men from the armory, jostled around getting in line under the pines. Lieutenant Mainus their Company commander walked among them. Private Millsass of this company looked out across the valley to where the Union troops were preparing to meet them. The Southerners could make out blue forms scurrying about preparing for them.

Down the line, Captain Elliott's Company D of the Athen's Battalion was ready to move out. Private John Chancy with his rifle shouldered, waited. From the city of Athens, Lieutenant Middlebrook waited for the command to advance. Men were quiet in their thoughts and moved their feet in line to keep warm. What Georgia troops had bayonets shoved them down on their rifle barrels and clicked them in place.

To the Athens troops immediate left, the Augusta Battalion stood in line waiting. Captain Adams Company B, stood in line with his men. There wasn't much to do from a soldiers point of view but wait. He stood near Lt. G. P. Weigle of his company and they, like the rest of the Georgia troops, looked across at the blue battle lines on the far side of the field. The Southerners stood there knowing that there would be lines of waiting infantry with their muskets aimed at them from behind those Union entrenchments.

Nearby Company C, with their Commander, Capt. A. T. Smith, was in line and anxiously waiting. Pvts. Jerry Gleason and J. D. Andrews, both of Augusta, stared at the Union fortifications eight hundred yards away from where they stood. They could see the dry brown corn stalks still standing in some of the field to their front. The corn stalks swayed in the cold November wind.

The Redding brothers, Pvts. William and James, with their gray cotton uniforms wet and heavy with the sleet and snow that had been falling off and on all day, stepped in line with their formation. The boys had thoughts of their mother, Maria, now waiting for them at home in Monroe County and of their father Capt. Dan Redding serving elsewhere in the Confederate army.

Sixteen year old Pvt. J. J. Eckles re-arranged his thick home-woven blanket that he had been carrying over his shoulder since leaving home with his unit. It was cold and he would need it to keep him warm tonight. He decided to bring it with him and not leave it on the ground in the tree line as some of the other soldiers had done. Private Eckles surveyed the field to his front. He could make out the Union troops entrenched on the crest. He then formed line with the others from his company.

The men and boys who had just passed through the destroyed Griswoldville knew what was at stake today. Some of the officers gave short addresses to their units exhorting them to do their duty. Their homes and loved ones were depending upon what they did that day. If this battle could be won, their county or city or even Georgia itself would be saved from the torch and insults of the Union army. The young boys and men listened to their officers and steeled themselves for what was yet to come on the field in front of them.7

Lieutenant Colonel B. D. Evans and his State Line troops formed in line. They wouldn't have long to wait before advancing across the field to the blue line on the opposite crest. Colonel Evans would report, "I had been in line but a few moments before ordered to advance and attack the enemy in front..."[8]

General Phillips, among his troops in the pines, looked out across the field. He then turned his eyes and watched his fellow Georgians dressed right, line after line, for one mile across. Phillips turned and gave the order to charge. The brigades moved through the pines in good order to reach the edge of the field.

The first Confederate line burst into the open field, its colors fluttering in the breeze. The long gray line stretched out across the open expanse for one mile. The Georgian line was over a thousand strong as they advanced. The men kept an unbroken front as they moved irresistibly forward into the corn field in quick step. Some of the Confederate officers advanced on horseback with their commands. Colonel Evans, after emerging from the pines, looked to his right expecting to see Major Cook's two battalions coming on with his men. All he saw was an open field. The surprised Colonel Evans turned his eyes back to the front and with his State Line troops continued to advance.[9]

Major Cook's two battalions were slow to move from the pines. Because his command was far to the right, the order to charge arrived after the others in General Smith's force were already advancing down the slope. When General Cook's men did advance, because of their obtuse position in the line, they had to march toward the State Line troops and then they had to wheel to the right toward the enemy and join up with Colonel Evans' State Line ranks to their left. Later Colonel Evans would report that, "We charged down through the old field alone, but were soon supported handsomely by Maj. Cook and Maj. Jackson, on my right."[10]

General Anderson advanced with his brigade down the hill. Capt. John J. McArthur of Anderson's Brigade tried to keep his 26 men of Company C, 7th Regiment, in line as they charged through the open field brushing aside the brown corn stalks.

Private Christopher Bier held the colors high as he and his fellow Georgians moved across the open field with the Athen's Battalion "keeping a fine line..." as later reported by Lt. Col. B.

D. Evans. [11]

On the opposite side of the valley, Union Lt. Charles W. Wills looked across the field and was astonished to see, some eight hundred yards away in the open field, "...By the time their first line had got within 250 yards of us, three other lines had emerged from the woods and they had run two batteries out on the field."[12]

Still standing by the big pine tree on the crest of the hill, General Walcutt rubbed his shoulder where he had been severely wounded earlier in the war at Shiloh. In fact the Confederate piece of lead was still in his shoulder, it had never been removed. As he viewed the advancing enemy he realized that the Confederates were coming on to drive them from the hill. He began issuing orders. He ordered Major Johnson, 100th Indiana Regiment to send three of his companies from the left of the line to the center of the line, to help defend Arndt's Battery. Again he ordered the troops to hold their fire. The battery was ordered to return fire when ready. Then General Walcutt stepped behind the large pine and peered out to the advancing enemy, lost in his thoughts. He watched the Confederate line coming on in fields of gray. Their colors were streaming in the cold breeze. A mile line of muskets were coming at his line in quick step formation. The Georgians pressed into the corn fields pushing the stalks aside as they advanced.[13]

Major Johnson of the 100th Indiana Regiment, upon receiving General Walcutt's order, sent companies I, K, and H, under the command of Capt. John W. Headington, to support Arndt's Battery in the center of the line.[14]

The thick bearded Captain of the Confederate artillery, Ruel Anderson again ordered his batteries into action to support the advancing gray line. Lt. Henry Greaves began firing his Napoleon guns in the direction of the center of the line and the Union battery.[15]

Union Captain Albert Arndt decided at this crucial time to move one of his Rodman guns to a new position to create a crossfire. As the artillerymen tried to clear a path for the gun, General Phillips' Confederates had already begun their charge across the field. As the Northerners struggled with the gun, a Confederate shell from Lt. Henry Greaves' guns, some 800 yards away, smashed into a caisson. Captain Arndt went down with what some of his men thought a mortal wound. The Union battery was thrown into confusion at the exact time it was needed most to wreck havoc on the Georgians in the open field. The Federal battery continued to "feebly engaged" the charging troops and the opposing enemy battery.16

Lieutenant Charles W. Wills must have been a little apprehensive as he noted in his dairy, "...Our artillery was silenced almost immediately."17

The second Confederate line, composed mostly of militia, now stepped smartly from the trees and joined the first line moving into the open field. They too were more than a thousand strong. As they advanced their feet and fingers stung from the cold and their wet clothing weighed heavily on their backs. The Georgia clay stuck to their shoes like soft red bricks. It was as if the clay was trying to hold them fast to the ground and not let them advance into danger. Still the Georgians came on following their colors across the open field.18

The tan, lean, farm boys from the Midwest on the opposite crest, glanced nervously at General Walcutt, who remained silent, still peering from behind the great pine tree at the advancing gray lines of the enemy. The troops fully expected him to order the command to fire. But the general stared ahead, not acknowledging his own men glancing at him.19

Adjutant Fenwick Hedley of the 32nd Illinois would describe General Sherman's soldiers in his diary, "they were veterans who had served an apprenticeship of more than three years at their profession and learned nearly all that was worth knowing." These veteran troops were staring down the hill at the advancing gray lines coming on at a charge straight at their position.20

The third Southern line now poured out from the green pine trees, flags unfurled fluttering and snapping in the cold breeze Officers could be heard barking out orders as the men moved into the open field. Close it up, close it up, keep the lines, forward the officers shouted. Now all three gray lines were in the open field, each one reaching nearly a mile across. Each line advancing forward into the 190 acre expanse that separated the two forces. The clean shaven Georgia Brig. Gen. H. K. McCay stepped out with men from his 4th Brigade, Georgia Militia, made up of the 10th, 11th, and 12th Regiments, Georgia Militia.

All three lines were now clearly in view of the waiting Union troops on the hill. Lieutenant Charles W. Wills, in the Union line with the 103rd Illinois, would later say, "We all felt we had a sure thing, and had there been but one line of rebels, we would have let them come up close to us."[21]

The three Southern lines were drawing closer to the Federal entrenchments. The troops in the first Georgian line jumped the first small stream they came to about four hundred yards from the Union lines. The first gray line was now half the way to the enemies line on the crest. They forged across a hard packed clay road that cut across the open farm field, the clay weighing heavily on their shoes as they continued to advance.

Anderson's Battery on the north side of the railroad was still actively supporting the advancing Confederate lines. They had been peppering the enemy with shot to keep their infantrymen pinned down. Now all four Napoleons began a barrage of the crest firing about three shots a minute. Shells began exploding along the Union entrenchments.

Colonel James N. Mann's 2nd Brigade, held in reserve, watched their friends, neighbors and relatives and their fellow Georgians, in the advancing three gray lines to their front. They could hear officers shouting out orders to keep the lines straight. Orders urging the troops to fill in the ranks and always the order to keep moving. They watched as their fellow Georgians kept their lines moving forward with their cold numb fingers clutching muskets, swords, pistols and their flags, advancing with courage and vigor.[22]

The second line now forged over the small stream four hundred yards from the enemy. The sounds of artillery mixed with officers shouting orders and the clanking of sabers and rifles could be heard as the gray lines drew closer to the crest.

The advancing Georgians began to realize that only a weak

desultory fire was coming from the Union battery located in the center of the line on the crest of the hill. It wasn't affecting the Southern advance at all and more importantly the Union muskets were still silent along the crest of the hill.23

General Phillips watched his three-one mile long gray lines advancing across the field. He had also noticed that the counter fire of the enemies battery was weak. Since ordering the attack he could do nothing but watch and wait, as his men had done before the order to advance. He watched as the third line now pushed over the small stream located halfway to the Northern lines. Still no enemy rifle fire came from the crest.

As the gray lines were sweeping forward, Maj. Asias Willison of the 103rd Illinois Regiment, said it was so quiet at this point of the battle, "He could hear rebel officers calling commands."24

Union Colonel Robert Catterson of the 97th Indiana Regiment would write in his official report, "The Brigade, thus posted behind a light barricade...lay anxiously awaiting his appearance...He (the enemy) was soon discovered emerging from the woods about 800 yards from our position and rapidly running across an open field toward us in three lines of battle, either of which more than covered our brigade front."25

When the first Southern line was about 250 yards away, the men looking to General Walcutt, finally got the command they had been waiting for. General Walcutt gave the order to fire. A heavy volley from the Union line tore into the gray ranks. Men and boys went down. Screams and moans came from the broken Southern line as the heavy fire tore limbs from bodies, shattered bones and splattered their blood on the field. Bullets began ripping into the dry corn stalks cutting them down like a giant scythe. The first line looked surprise at this intense fire. "They", one soldier would say, "halted, wavered, and appeared amazed." The officers rallied their Georgia troops in the field, reformed and they continued to come on. Shouts of fill the ranks, fill the ranks, close up, could be heard.26

Lieutenant Charles W. Wills would write that, "We then let loose on them with our muskets, and one after another their lines crumbled to pieces, and they ran. Our little brigade had 1,100 muskets engaged, while the rebels had about 6,000." He would go on to explain, "but the four brigades were militia." The Georgians may have run at this point but they were running forward toward the protection of the branch.27

In Anderson's Brigade, men of Captain John J. McArthur's Company C began to go down. 1st Lt. Gipp Wilcox was hit in the thigh and Pvt. Thomas B. Adams would take a bullet in the hand. Pvt. Groves Connor would never see his home county of Montgomery, he would die advancing with his Georgia 7th Regiment. Captain McArthur's Company C was down to 23 men as they as they continued to move forward.28

Anderson's Battery was having a telling effect on the Union battery damaging one of Arndt's cannons. Captain Arndt had rejoined his command after suffering only a severe bruise. Half of his fourteen artillerists had been wounded, several with arms and legs missing. Half of his artillery pieces also were put out of the action. Six of his artillery horses were down, other horses were engaged in taking wounded to the rear. Finally to save the complete destruction of his guns Captain Arndt had them pulled from the field to the rear of the action. The Northern artillery was now out of commission and the battle had only begun.29

While the Confederate battery was having great success, the gray infantry lines were being ripped apart by the Union rifle fire. But in spite of the heavy Federal infantry fire, the Georgians kept moving forward. The lines of gray clad infantry seemed to have a life of its own, wavering under heavy fire, bloodied, they would regroup then surge forward. One of the first wounded was Pvt. Henry Mercer, of Wilkinson County. As he went down, Capt. A. A. Beall of his company (apparently without a rifle), seized his musket and moved forward. Elsewhere along the line, one of the Redding brothers, Pvt. William Redding, was hit and crumpled to the ground. He was left to die among the cornstalks of his native state.30

Federal bullets continued to cut the cornstalks and bushes to the ground, making a snapping sound as they hit. Some of the Northern units were using the new Spencer repeating rifles to great effect. Although they were outnumbered three to one by the Southerners, they had tremendous fire power with the new rifles. Their rapid fire was directed down toward the branch and had a much better chance of finding flesh and bone than the Georgians did by having to fire up the hill.[31]

Private Upson would later write in his diary,

> we had but slight works thrown up hastily
> with rails, but we had one thing that helped us
> greatly and that was part of our men are armed
> with repeating rifles which enabled us to keep a
> continuous fire. We really had only 1,513 men
> in line, including two guns of a Battery, while
> the Johnys had a least 4 and probably 5 times
> that number- also, a full Battery of 6 guns which
> they handled well...[32]

The Confederate infantrymen firing that went high wouldn't go unnoticed by the Northerners. Lt. Charles Wills of the 103rd Illinois, estimated that ten of every dozen bullets fired by the enemy flew high overhead. Two of those dozen bullets were coming into the lines and some Federals began to fall. The Union wounded were continually being helped to the rear.[33]

The big pine tree located in the center of the branch was constantly being hit with bullets and minnie balls. Soldiers nearby could hear the snap of the branches and thuds as the bullets found a mark on the tree trunk. The tree had survived countless years in the branch but would it survive that day.[34]

The noise from more than 7,000 weapons firing in this 190 acre battlefield must have been deafening for the troops involved. Many reports of "heavy and galling fire" were made after the battle.[35]

Meanwhile the frontal assault envisioned by General Phillips wasn't working to his plan. Colonel Evans' State Line force that had been joined by Major Cook's two battalions on his right were both receiving a "galling and destructive fire from the entire line," Lt. Col. Evans would later write. Lt. Col. Beverly Evans kept his men moving toward the protection of the branch. He saw some of his men go down in the line and their places taken by others. Ranks of Georgians continued to fill in the gaps torn by Northern bullets. The State Line troops would suffer 52 casualties with only three killed in the fighting. More than 150 yards from the branch and just after crossing over the small clay road that dissected the battlefield, Lt. Colonel Evans himself would suffer a wound. Although wounded he continued to advance with his men to the safety of the thicket. Lt. Colonel Evans would stay on the battlefield, but his injury would force him to relinquish his command. He was replaced as commander of the Georgia State Line troops by Lt. Col. James Wilson.[36]

Smoke from the cannon and rifle-fire began to drift across the battlefield. The State Line men were opposed in the Union line by the 6th Iowa, three companies of the 100th Indiana and the left part of the 103rd Illinois. Some of these troops were the ones manning the remnants of the farm buildings they had torn down for material and used for the construction of their entrenchments. From these buildings the Federals continued to fire at the State Line troops advancing toward them. From their position they helped slow and then break up the Confederate attack directed toward the center of the Union line.[37]

For a time the Confederate shells of Anderson's Battery played havoc along the breast works scattering deadly splinters. An Iowa soldier later recalled that a single shell hit the rail barrier, "where the regimental colors were waving." It killed the color bearer, "blowing the top of his head off and saturating the colors with his blood," and also severely wounded eight of his comrades. The 6th Iowa Regiment continued to fight on under their bloody colors.[38]

When the first line of Confederates reached the Big Sandy Creek Branch, Colonel Mann unleashed his 2nd Brigade, Georgia Militia. They were General Phillips' only reserve. A row of guns and colors that had been hidden in the pines now came streaming forward to join their fellow Georgians in the rain of fire. The entire 2nd Brigade consisting of the 4th, 5th and 6th Regiments came on at a run. Close up, close up, barked the officers. "The first line of battle having reached the branch," Colonel Mann would say later, "I ordered the 2nd Brigade of

Georgia Militia into the battle where they supported the State Line troops and the 4th Brigade." Four lines of Georgia infantry, composed entirely of militia, was now bearing down on the Union entrenchments. At this point in the battle, General Phillips now had no reserve to take advantage of any break, if it were to happen, in the Union lines.[39]

Later General Phillips' report would describe this unorthodox move by Colonel Mann who commanded Phillips' own brigade, "Colonel Mann, deeming that his Brigade could be of more service near the lines, advanced it to near the same position, where it participated in the general action."[40]

On the far left of the Confederate line, the slender, bearded General Anderson realized his attack had gotten off to a bad start. Instead of staying north of the railroad and over-lapping then slamming into the Federal far right, Anderson's men had veered to their right, crossing over to the southern side of the railroad. They were now opposite the center of the Union line, manned by the 103rd Illinois Regiment. A small unit of Anderson's command, when moving forward in the initial attack, had gotten cut off and stayed on the north side of the railroad.

General Phillips' report later stated,

> From some misconception of orders, when the general advance was being made General Anderson's brigade faced to the right and swept across the railroad (save a small detachment on his extreme left that was cut off by a deep cut in the railroad) and participated with the State Line and General McCay's brigade in the direct attack, where they, both officers and men, sustained themselves with decision and gallantry.[41]

When the State Line troops of Lt. Colonel Evans' command had reached the main branch they stopped and delivered a volley into the farm buildings to their front. They had been receiving a deadly harassing fire from the Northerners there which had been tearing gaps in their gray lines.[42]

The Union troops in the farm buildings were still delaying Lt. Colonel Evans' State Line troops attack on the center of General Walcutt's line. Now his State Line troops were becoming mixed with other commands on both of his flanks. Lt. Col. James Wilson, now in command of the State Line, moved his men forward across the branch under the slope of the next hill where he again halted, "firing on the enemy's front, causing them to abandon the houses and take refuge behind their works," Lt. Colonel Evans would later write in his official report.43

After clearing the Union troops from the farm buildings, the elite State Line troops were surprised when they began receiving fire from the thickets to their rear. This fire came from the Confederate's second line, composed of Georgia militiamen. They had just arrived at the branch and in the thickening smoke assumed the State Line troops were the enemy and let loose a volley on them. This produced a temporary confusion among the beleaguered State Line troops before the firing finally could be stopped and order restored.44

Almost all of General Phillips' force was now bearing down on the center and right-center of the Union line. The 103rd Illinois, 6th Iowa, 40th Illinois Regiments and the three detached companies of the 100th Indiana Regiment would be hard pressed over the next few hours of fighting. The gray wave of Southern infantry would continually lap at the right center of the union entrenchments trying to find an opening.45

Union General Walcutt, upon seeing this, began shifting more men to the right side of the line to counter the deployment of the Georgians as they surged forward. A command was sent to Lt. Colonel Alexander moving his 46th Ohio Regiment to the far right to strengthen that side of the Federal line.46

Major Ruel Johnson, 100th Indiana Regiment, was then ordered to again detach three more companies of his regiment and move them to the far right of the Union line where he was to take command of that portion of the defense. His order from General Walcutt was to, "at all hazards hold the enemy at bay at that point."47

Major Ruel Johnson pulled Companies A, B, and C, rushing

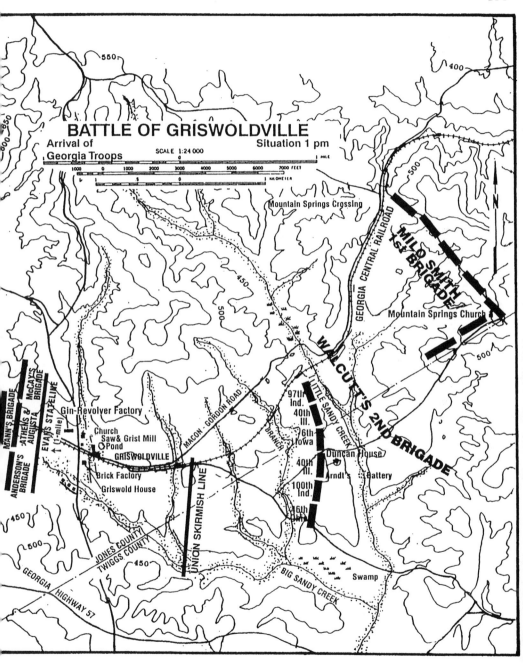

BATTLE OF GRISWOLDVILLE

Arrival of
Georgia Troops

Situation 1 pm

SCALE 1:24 000

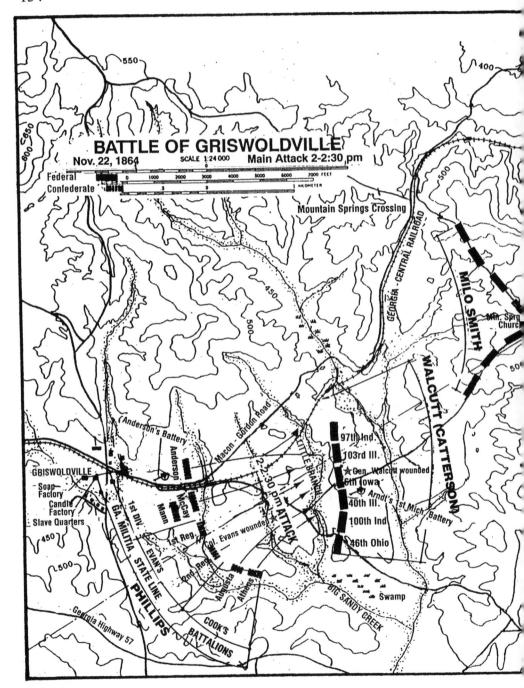

BATTLE OF GRISWOLDVILLE
Nov. 22, 1864   SCALE 1:24 000   Main Attack 2-2:30 pm

Federal
Confederate

Mountain Springs Crossing

GEORGIA - CENTRAL RAILROAD

MILO SMITH

Mtn. Sprg Church

WALCUTT (CATTERSON)

Anderson's Battery

Anderson

Macon - Gordon Road

LITTLE BRANCH

97th Ind.

103rd Ill.

★Gen. Walcutt wounded

6th Iowa

Arndt's 1st Mich. Battery

40th Ill.

100th Ind

46th Ohio

GRISWOLDVILLE

Soap Factory

Candle Factory

Slave Quarters

1st DIV.

McCay

Mann

1st Reg.

Col. Evans wounded

2-2:30 pm ATTACK

GA. MILITIA STATE LINE

EVANS

2nd Reg.

Augusta

Athens

BIG SANDY CREEK

Swamp

PHILLIPS

COOK'S

BATTALIONS

Georgia Highway 57

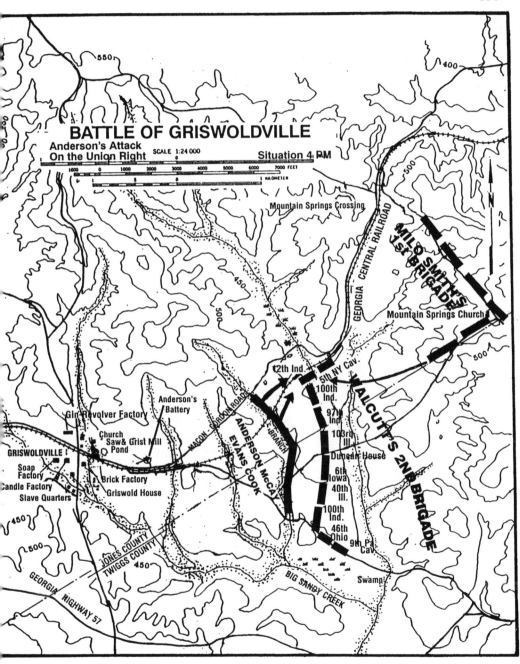

BATTLE OF GRISWOLDVILLE

Anderson's Attack
On the Union Right

SCALE 1:24 000

Situation 4 PM

1000   0   1000   2000   3000   4000   5000   6000   7000 FEET

1   0   .5   0   .5   1 KILOMETER

Mountain Springs Crossing

GEORGIA CENTRAL RAILROAD

MILO SMITH'S 1st BRIGADE

Mountain Springs Church

2th Ind.

5th NY Cav.
100th Ind.

WALCUTT'S 2ND BRIGADE

97th Ind.

103rd Ill.

Duncan House

6th Iowa
40th Ill.

100th Ind.

46th Ohio

9th P. Cav.

Anderson's Battery

Gin Revolver Factory

ANDERSON McCAY
EVANS COOK

MACON - GORDON ROAD

L. BRANCH

Church
Saw & Grist Mill
Pond

GRISWOLDVILLE

Soap Factory

Candle Factory

Slave Quarters

Brick Factory

Griswold House

JONES COUNTY
TWIGGS COUNTY

GEORGIA HIGHWAY 57

BIG SANDY CREEK

Swamp

them to the far right. He put Companies A, and C, on line and put Company B out to the right as skirmishers to extend his line further right. Major Johnson told his men to, " shelter behind trees and to hold the position at all hazards." Major Johnson had four remaining Companies of the 100th Indiana Regiment, D, E, F, and G which now had to occupy the line previously held by his entire regiment and the 46th Ohio had held. He spread the men out across the two regimental front as best as he could and put Capt. John Headington in command of that portion of the line.48

Colonel Catterson would write of the Southern advance, "On came the enemy, endeavoring to gain possession of a ravine running parallel to and about 100 yards to our front, but the fire was so terrible that ere he reached it many of his number were stretched upon the plain. It was at this moment that General Walcutt received a severe wound and was compelled to leave the field."49

Union General Charles Walcutt after issuing orders to move the troops to the far right was knocked down by a shell burst from Anderson's Confederate battery some 800 yards distance across the field. He was painfully wounded in the lower part of one leg when a shell fragment ripped a two ounce piece of flesh from it. General Walcutt was borne off the battlefield by his troops. He would see no further action on that day.50, 51

Colonel Robert Catterson, fighting with his 97th Indiana Regiment, about 150-200 yards to the right of where General Walcutt went down, would be sent for to take command of the 2nd Brigade in the thick of the fighting. He immeadiatly realized what General Walcutt had known before being wounded, that the extreme right of the Union line was being threaten by the advancing Confederate infantry. Colonel Catterson would write in his official report,

> I supposed he contemplated turning my right
> flank. As I had already disposed of every
> available man in the brigade, and my left being
> so strongly pressed that not a man could be

spared from it, I sent to the general commanding
the division for two regiments.52

Major Asias Willison, 103rd Illinois Regiment, reported, "As
soon as they (the Georgia troops) came within range of our
muskets, a most terrific fire was poured into their ranks, doing
fearful execution...still they moved forward."53
As the Confederates reached the safety of the branch they
began to reform. One of them, sixteen year old Pvt. J. J. Eckles,
sat down in the clay exhausted as soon as he was out of sight of
the enemy. As bullets whizzed around him he unrolled the thick
home-woven blanket he had carried over his shoulder, shook out
some misshapen lead pellets, and counted twenty-seven bullet
holes in the cloth. It was a grim testament to the heavy firing
coming from the Union line.54
Among the brambles, small trees and briars the Georgians regrouped and surged forward to within one hundred yards of the
Northern line. Shouts of forward boys could be heard as soldiers
fell in the clay, their dirty gray uniforms now stained in blood.
Some of the wounded would lay in the protection of the ravine as
the battle swirled about them. Above the noise of the battle, the
gray lines rippled under the constant Union fire before once
again being driven back to the branch. In some parts of the line
they came even closer. Maj. Asias Willison, 103rd Illinois
Regiment in the right center of the Union line, reports, "...they
moved forward, and came within 45 yards of our works. Here
they attempted to reform their line, but so destructive was the fire
that they were compelled to retire." This attack had ground to a
halt as the Georgians pulled back to the cover and safety of the
ravine.55
The Confederates fired from behind the undergrowth which
provided protection from Union bullets. Nearby in the red
Georgia clay lay Pvt. James Redding bleeding to death. He had
suffered a mortal wound. Maria Searcy Redding, at home in
Monroe County, would lose both of her sons on this dark day.56
Union Lt. Charles W Wills, 103rd Illinois Regiment, would
later remember, "It was awful the way we slaughtered those

men."[57]

In Confederate Colonel Mann's 2nd Brigade sector of the advance, thirteen year old Pvt. Bridges Smith and fourteen year old Pvt. W. A. Poe huddled in vicinity of the branch as the firing swirled around them. Men of Colonel Mann's 2nd Brigade and General Anderson's 3rd Brigade where mixing together on Mann's left. On his 2nd Brigade's right, his troops were mingling with Lt. Col. Beverly Evans' State Line soldiers. Pvts. Smith and Poe picked up their muskets again and moved forward with the rest of their company as the order was given again to try and take the Union line. Colonel Mann stepped forward from the protection of the ravine with his men when he was struck by a bullet and wounded. Colonel Mann's 2nd Brigade (General Phillips' own brigade) would suffer heavily in the days action.[58] In the 2nd Brigade 13 would die, 115 would be wounded and 28 would be listed as missing in action.[59]

A soldier in Colonel Mann's Brigade, Felix Pryor, would describe the fierce fighting in a letter to his wife Nancy,

> ...Several of our company were wounded but none killed dead on the battlefield. Colonel Mann and lieutenant-Colonel Bowdoin of our regiment were both wounded. Seaborn Walker (was) wounded severely in the thigh. Porer Fears (was) wounded, George Stovall slightly in the neck. Mr. Zachery in leg. Mr. Burroughs slightly grazing skin on top of his head. Joe Few, Jr. slightly. Several others of our company were slightly touched with balls and not hurt much. Several of my acquaintances in the regiment were killed and others severely wounded. I escaped without being touched though two or three were struck close by me and severely wounded.[60]

Other Confederates along the branch would continually surge forward. Gray clad bodies tumbled into the mud as others took their places in the line moving into the hail of lead. Litter bearer, Pvt. William Caswell, Company H, saw a man fall clutching his wound. Private Caswell ran to him, bending down to help the wounded man he felt a sharp pain in both of his hips and he too went down. Passing the wounded Private Caswell, Captain Adams, Company H, continued to move his men forward, trying to reach the Federal entrenchments. To some, "It seemed that no living thing could cross that hail of shot and shell which was poured into them as they charged up that slope."[61]

The veteran Union infantrymen began to suspect by now that these rebels had never seen battle. They came on too bravely, heedless of exposure or losses. The Federal units with their repeating rifles fired so rapidly that most regiments ran low on ammunition and drummer boys had to run to the rear for more cartridges for the new hungry rifles. Luckily for the Union troops, the ammunition wagons had arrived near the Federal lines in spite of the fact that some of the mule teams had been cut down by fire from Anderson's Battery. Fire from the Union lines began to noticeably slacken. Men in the Federal line, without an order being given by their officers, began to calmly fix bayonets. The Federals, bayonets at the ready, waited for the Confederates to leap over the breastworks. The Northerners also notice the reduced firing coming from their own lines. Private Upson, 100th Indiana Regiment, would write in his diary, "once when we where so hard pressed that it seemed as though they were going to run over us by sheer force of numbers our boys put on their bayonets resolved to hold their ground at any cost."[62]

Men of the 100th Indiana Regiment expressed their determination to hold their line as long as there was a man of them left. Officers were running up and down the line cheering their men on and urging them to hold their ground and beat back the enemy moving ever closer to their entrenchments. Major Johnson would report after the fighting that the 100th Indiana Regiment, "suffered 2 men killed and 18 wounded."[63]

General Phillips didn't know it but his best opportunity to break the blue line had arrived and was slowly slipping away. Again the southern line swept to within 50 to 100 yards of the

entrenchments before the Union drummer boys came along
handing out cartridges. The young drummer boys were furiously
opening boxes as the Confederates worked their way closer to the
fortified line. The volleys of Union fire began to increase again.
The Southern lines now noticeably thinner with fewer colors in
the line, wavered, then stalled, falling back once more to the
safety of the ravine. The thin blue line on the crest had held
again. But how many more attacks could it beat back?[64]

Private's "Uncle" Aaron Wolford and Theodore Upson, 100th
Indiana Regiment, were firing side by side behind the
breastworks, when Pvt. Wolford slumped to the ground with a
mortal wound to his head. The boy put a hand on the old man's
shoulder. "Uncle Aaron! Oh, Uncle Aaron." He was dead.
Private Upson hoped his friend, "...was gone where I hope there
are no wars, no sudden partings." Private Upson also thought of
his friends wife, "who will see him no more."[65]

On the extreme right of the Southern advance, after a slow
beginning, Major Cook's men had made it to the thicket of the
branch. Here the officers regrouped their men. Major Cook's
Battalions had pinched into the center of the line and would be
advancing against the 40th Illinois Regiment with the main part
of his force and not their intended target, the weak left of the
Union line. Here a few of Major Cook's men from Athens and
Augusta made only one weak attack against the 46th Ohio
Regiment before General Walcutt had pulled them from the line
and moved them to the far right. Lieutenant Colonel Alexander
of the 46th Ohio Regiment said, "...they were allowed to come
within thirty yards before orders were given to fire; they were
easily repulsed. They left upon the field a number of horses
which had been killed and disabled and one prisoner." Only four
companies of the 100th Indiana Regiment stretched across the
two regimental front. Hitting at this part of the line, Major
Cook's Battalions would have most likely cracked the Union line
and then rolled them up from left to right. For some unknown
reason, Major Cook would never compensate for pinching in
toward the center of the Confederate line. The attack, as ordered
by General Phillips, that could have meant a Southern victory,

never materialized on the Union left. The four companies of the 100th Indiana Regiment spread across a two regimental front would never be hard pressed throughout the entire battle.66

Major Nichols, General Sherman's Aide-de-Camp, would write he also felt the enemy were new troops,

> The enemy ...advanced upon our troops who had thrown up temporary breastworks...with the ignorance of danger common to new troops...rushed upon our veterans with the greatest fury...our soldiers firing coolly, while shouting derisively to the quivering columns to come on, as if they thought the whole thing a nice joke. The Rebels resumed the, attack, but with the same fatal results...67

Lieutenant Mainus moved his men of Company B of the Athens Battalion, the workers from the armory, forward from the branch. They were around 150 yards from the enemy entrenchments when they burst from the thickets. Union fire immediately started taking its toll. Lieutenant Mainus was slightly wounded, Pvt. M. R. Baggs took a slug in his arm, Pvt. James Brane took a bullet in his mouth, blood poured from his lips. Pvt. H. U. Durham fell to the ground clutching a wound to his stomach as blood seeped from his shirt and jacket. What men were able, of Company B, continued to move forward firing as they advanced into the smoke toward the Federal lines.68

The fire from the 103rd Illinois Regiment was damaging to the advancing Georgians. The Athens and Augusta Battalions advanced as far as they could into the punishing fire. Major Cook's Battalions fell back to the protection of the thicket at the branch to try and regroup. Major Cook also realized his men were mixing with men of the State Line troops, located to their left in the ravine.

Private Christopher Bier, advancing with the colors toward the opposite crest of the hill felt a pain in his wrist. He had been hit by a Union bullet and wouldn't advance any further against the

Federal line. If the colors were to be planted on the enemy's entrenchments that day, Private Bier wouldn't be the one to do it. Nearby, Pvt. J. A. Moody, his hands already numb from the cold, looked down to his hand and noticed his finger had been shot off. He tried to stem the flow of blood from his hand as he withdrew from the field.[69]

On the battlefield, Company B of the Athens Battalion, located on the far right of the Southern line, was taking heavy casualties. Lt. J. H. Hunter was down with a mortal wound. Private C. Clearland was brought down by Northern bullets and left dying, his blood mixing with the red Georgia clay. Private Millsass received wounds in both thighs and had to be helped back to the Confederate line.[70]

Many Confederate wounded lay on the cold, wet, Georgia mud and clay throughout the battle. Some not receiving help for hours. Others would be exposed to the cold throughout the night before help would come the next morning. Others would be helped to the safety of the ravine. The galling fire of the Union infantry tore gaps in the Athens and Augusta Battalion's lines. With their colors hesitating, Major Cook's men again began withdrawing back to the security of the ravine.

The Georgians from Augusta and Athens didn't spend too long in the ravine before they moved forward again to try and dislodge the 103rd Illinois Regiment from the crest. Shouts of, forward boys, could be heard over the din of musket and cannon fire as they came on again. Men from Company D, Athens Battalion, broke from the gall-bushes in the branch and were immeadiatly hit with Union fire. Pvt. John Chancey took a slug and fell to the cold Georgia mud, dead. Lieutenant Middlebrook leading his men forward would fall forward with a bullet to his knee that had shattered it. He would later have his leg sawed off by surgeons. Company C, Athens Battalion, would later list seven of its numbers missing and presumed dead. They were Pvts. S. Bassett, J. Beall, R. Beall, J. Cawthre, A. D. Snow, O. Stone and W. R. Tanny. Company C would be one of Major Cook's companies to suffer the most during the action.[71]

Major Jackson's Augusta Battalion to the left of the Athens

Battalion, advanced shoulder to shoulder up the slope with their brother Georgians. Colors flying, they moved against the hard pressed 103rd Illinois Regiment, some 150 yards away. As proof of the galling fire in which they lost heavily that day, the *Augusta Daily Constitutionalist* would later report, "...as an evidence of the storm of leaden hail they passed through, the colors of the Augusta Battalion bears the mark of sixteen Federal Bullets."[72]

Company A, Athens Battalion, advanced into the devastating fire. Pvt. John Copeland suffered a slight foot wound, and Pvt. William Churchill felt a jarring pain as a lead slug slammed him hard in the shoulder. Nearby in Company C, Lieutenant Poole was hit seriously in the head and had to be helped back. A slug slammed into the shoulder of Private Gaunt. Pvt. Jerry Gleason stopped a bullet in the leg and limped back from the action. Four privates of this company would be listed as missing after the battle, George Shiver, James Walker, M. P. Scales and John Scales. Fingers aching from the cold, the men from Athens fired their muskets at the Federal lines but to no avail. Although pressed hard by the Georgians, the left center of the Union breastworks would hold.[73]

Miraculously Major Cook's Augusta and Athens Battalions suffered only 5 killed in the battle, 63 wounded and 19 would later be listed as missing and probably dead in the action.[74]

The far left of the Union line, being held only by the four companies of the 100th Indiana Regiment under Capt. John Headington, had to fire to their right as Confederate Major Cook's men came up the hill. Captain Headington's Indianans were not pressed hard at all during the battle as they anchored the far left of the Union line. They were soon joined on the left by the 9th Pennsylvania Cavalry Regiment under the command of Col. Thomas Jordan which was part of Col. Eli Murray's 1st Brigade. They would be used to bolster the far left of the line, next to Captain Headington's weak detachment of men located against the swamp.[75]

General Phillips would later report,

The order to Major Cook (from some cause

which I am not aware) to turn the enemy's left
was never carried out, yet his command
participated fully in the action, deported
themselves gallantly, and, I regret to say,
suffered much from wounds and deaths.

Major Cook's attack was still hitting mostly on the left center
of the Union line.[76]

The main Confederate push at present and the greatest threat
to the Federal line would come on the far right where General
Anderson was now re-organizing his attack. He ordered his
officers of the 3rd Brigade to get their men moving to their left in
the direction of the railroad. One of Lt. Col. Beverly Evans'
regiments, the 2nd, inadvertently followed General Anderson's
3rd Brigade as it moved to the far left, probably due to the
confusion the smoke and of being fired on from the rear by their
own men. As these troops moved to the left they created a gap in
the center of Lt. Colonel Evans' line that eventually was filled by
the advancing militia of the second line who had just unloaded
their muskets on the State Line troops. They poured into the
ravine and began firing at the Northern lines.[77]

In Macon, at 4:00 p.m. Thomas Hardeman, Assistant
Adjutant-General was writing out this command to General
Phillips,

I am directed by the major-general to instruct
you to withdraw your troops immediately to
some convenient camp this side of the Cross
Keys and take a suitable position for the night,
unless you receive further orders. You will leave
your camp this side of the Cross Keys at daylight to-morrow morning and come back to the
fortifications. Your note of 2 o'clock has been
received. Keep the courier who brings this until
you march, and notify us accordingly. When
you leave to-morrow morning send a courier,
stating the time you begin your march for the
fortifications. Put your scouts well out to-night

upon all roads leading from Clinton; or if the
enemy mass upon you from any direction, fall
back to the lines of fortifications upon their
approach and immediately report the facts.
There is a good branch just this side of Walnut
Creek. Our cavalry were near Clinton this
morning, but are being pushed back by the
enemy.[78]

This order would go out at 4:30 p.m. At 4:30 p.m. the Battle
of Griswoldville was almost over.

Right then, at another branch, the Big Sandy Creek Branch,
not the Walnut Creek Branch, Brig. Gen. Pleasant J. Phillips'
Georgia command was fighting for its life. Phillips' entire
infantry force, save General Anderson's small detachment that
had isolated itself to the left on the far side of the tracks, was
now in the branch or vicinity.[79]

As General Charles Anderson's men moved toward their left,
the 2nd Regiment, State Line followed along. As the State Line
troops moved to their left, their right touched up against the
Union lines. "And poured a well-directed fire into their (Union)
ranks, causing them to exhibit some confusion." Lt. Colonel
Evans would later report of the action to his left, "The firing was
incessant."[80]

General Anderson finally managed to add the detachment that
had been cut off on the north side of the railroad to his advancing
force. With these fresh troops he tried to carry out his original
order of turning the right flank of the enemy. The Confederate
advance took them within yards of the detachment of the 100th
Indiana, the 46th Ohio and the 97th Indiana Regiments. Within
yards of the Union Line, they were punished with a withering
fire. General Phillips would report, "...when a most spirited and
desperate fight ensued, lasting some hour and a half or more."[81]

The Federals were thrown into momentary confusion as
General Anderson's men pounded into the Union right. The
Union troops on the right flank didn't have any fortifications so
most of them were exposed to the enemy fire. Major Johnson

commanding the 100th Indiana Regiment would report that, "the ground being rather favorable, I succeeded in checking the enemy so suddenly in his effort to turn our line that he did not afterward attempt seriously to get around our flank..."[82]

The 46th Ohio Regiment, which had come from the left of the line had passed to the right came under heavy fire. They were ordered to deploy to cover a space equal to about three times my own proper front. In this position the 46th Ohio Regiment hastily fortified. Colonel Alexander would report they were involved on the right where they repulsed the enemy in four assaults.[83]

As forty-eight year old Sgt. Blanton Nance, Company E, 7th Regiment in General Anderson's 3rd Brigade advanced, he felt a bullet slam into his shoulder and another hit him in the neck. He stumbled and fell to the wet ground. After the battle Sergeant Nance would be listed as missing in action. His company commander Captain Morgan would be slightly wounded but continue fighting. Captain Singleton was hit in the head with a bullet and he went down and was eventually helped from the field by his fellow Georgians.[84] Colonel Abner Redding leading his 7th Regiment, Georgia Militia, up the hill, was shot and killed, giving his last full measure of devotion to the Confederate cause on this lonely Georgia hillside. Fifty-four year old William Whatley was wounded twice but would survive the battle.[85]

Another officer, 2nd Lt. Walter T. McArthur of company C, would go down with a wound and be listed as missing after the battle. Pvt Alexander Gillis would also suffer a wound. Pvt. Addison McArthur would be killed by a Union bullet on the fields of Duncan's farm. Pvt. William Ryals would also die in the attack on the Federal position. Captain McArthur's Company C would be down to 19 men by the end of the days fighting at Griswoldville. The company from Montgomery County would suffer three killed and four wounded out of the original 26 men that went into action on that day.[86]

In the 8th Regiment Pvt. William Jolly was killed among the brown stubble of cornstalks in the Georgia field. Private Jolly's blood drained away into the red clay of his home state. Another member of Private Jolly's company, Lt. John Baker was hit in the wrist. Trying to stem the blood, he retreated back off the field. As the firing grew heavier, Pvt. Wiley Vinson felt a pain in his side where a piece of lead had entered him and blood spurted out.[87]

The fighting was more fierce on the right side of the Union line. In this hail-storm of Union bullets the gallant Georgians led by the gallant General Anderson would surge from the safety of the ravine some seven times to try and wrest the crest of the hill from the Federals. Each attack would meet with the same bitter result, with the Georgians being driven back to the cover of the ravine. Maj. Ruel Johnson would later recall, "The enemy made seven distinct assaults upon our lines, and was handsomely repulsed with heavy loss on his part each time." The Union fire was unrelenting on the Southerners in front of their breastwork. The Confederates reciprocated with heavy fire of their own. In Union Major Johnson's line a Southern bullet every so often would find its mark and one of his 100th Indiana infantrymen would tumble to the earth writhing in pain.[88]

General Charles Anderson led his men forward one final time against the Union right only one hundred yards beyond the ravine. The men from Georgia fired their muskets as they tried to break the enemies line. Finally they could advance no further. The charge had come to a stop. Not able to go forward, not wanting to retreat, they stayed in their position. General Anderson halted his command and although their ammunition was nearly exhausted they held their ground just yards in front of the Federal entrenchments. From this position they slowly exchanged fire with the enemy at close range. Anderson's Brigade would fail to turn the Federal right. The last chance for a Southern victory slowly slipping away. Instead of a victory the Georgians would bleed to death in front of the Union lines. Anderson's Brigade would suffer 25 dead, 116 wounded and 22 missing. Many of the missing would later be found dead on the battlefield. This last chance for a victory had ground to a bloody halt just yards from the crest and the Union lines.[89]

General Phillips would write in his official report that,

After the action had progressed for some hours General Anderson took the detachment of his men that had been cut off, went round to the enemy's right flank, when a most spirited and desperate fight ensued, lasting some hour and a half or more; but the enemy was too firmly established and the General's force too small to dislodge him.[90]

With the temperature now dropping to below freezing, the ground was again hardening. The men couldn't even scoop dirt to form a pit for protection against the rain of Union bullets that were falling on them. The Confederate militiamen continued firing slowly till dark from behind any cover of scrub pine, gall bushes, and brush they could find. Lucky ones found a left over rail fence to fire from behind.[91]

In the attack General Anderson would attest to the heavy Union fire. He received two bullets through his clothes without causing a wound and a third that caused a severe wound to his hand. His official report would consist of two short terse paragraphs.[92]

Some of the Confederates on the far left pulled back to take shelter under cover of a ravine which ran along Major Johnson's 100th Indiana Regiment's front. From here they kept up a steady musket fire, most of it still going over the heads of the Union infantry on the crest.[93]

In this final advance near twilight, the gray line as it moved forward was thin. Undercover of darkness the Confederates began trying to take their wounded to the rear As they tried to remove the wounded, others moved slowly forward to distract the Union troops in the entrenchments. Remembering the humiliation of leaving wounded on the battlefield near Atlanta, the Georgia soldiers fought hard to remove them from this field of carnage. Under heavy enemy fire they carried most of the wounded from the field back toward Griswoldville. Doctor J. S. Henry in Company D, 9th Regiment, Georgia Militia was himself hit in the leg with a bullet slightly grazing him. He continued to administer to the wounded on the field.94

Elsewhere on the battlefield another bullet would find a Confederate doctor serving in the militia but he wouldn't be as lucky. Dr. J. A. Davis would become one of the casualties in the fighting at Griswoldville and die of bullet wounds suffered on that day.95

General Anderson's staff had also been hard hit during the days fighting. Captain Adams and Lieutenant Hamilton of his staff both suffered wounds in the fierce attacks.96

Lieutenant Colonel Evans' Georgia State Line troops were running low on ammunition, "...well-nigh exhausted," he would later report. His infantry kept up a steady fire on the Federal line.

Colonel Milo Smith's 12th Indiana Infantry Regiment under the command of a Major Baldwin arrived on the crest. Colonel Catterson rushed them to bolster the hard pressed right of the Union line. Col. Milo Smith in his report would tell of the arrival of this regiment just in time to help throw back General Anderson's attack, "One regiment-the Twelfth Indiana, Major Baldwin-moved on to the support of Second Brigade, and went into position on the right of the line, advanced skirmishers, meeting the enemy's skirmishers just in time to prevent them from flanking the Second Brigade. The Twelfth Indiana Regiment had one man slightly wounded." As the Twelfth Indiana Regiment swung into line under the direction of Adjt. Marshall H. Parks they watched as Parks tumbled from his horse to the Georgia mud. His horse had been shot dead from a Confederate bullet. The Indiana skirmishers advanced a short distance in front of the line when they became engaged with the men of General Anderson's Brigade. They again helped stop the Georgians attack on the far right of the Union line. As it was growing dark Colonel Catterson asked Col. Milo Smith for one additional regiment which was then added to the right of the Union line to help bolster it.97

The 5th Kentucky Cavalry Regiment also arrived under Colonel Baldwin's command. Colonel Catterson sent the Union horsemen to the far right flank to anchor the line facing the swamp. They were to help against the enemies attempt to turn their hard pressed right flank. Colonel Baldwin would later write in his report, "Late in the afternoon, my command was ordered to take position on the right of the infantry, then engaged in battle near Griswoldville, which position I occupied till dark, not becoming engaged, however."[98]

Lt. Henry Greaves limbered up his battery at the old number 18 train station and withdrew back to rejoin the rest of Anderson's Battery among the pines.

It was growing darker and colder. The wet clay began to freeze hard. The Confederates in the thickets at the branch could hear the cries of the wounded above the crackle of muskets. They had been under stiff fire from the Federals for almost three hours. Lt. Colonel Evans would call it, "a hail-storm of bullets." For over three hours the Georgians had tried to crack the Union line to no avail. The blue wall would go unbroken on that day.[99]

Finally with darkness coming on, Brigadier General Phillips had had enough. He ordered his command to retire from the field. He realized his attack had ground to a halt. Nothing could now be accomplished by continuing the attack into the darkness. As the Confederates pulled back, one soldier would notice that, "there was not a bush or cornstalk left on the hill." In the dusk, what men remained, walked, limped and crawled back to Griswoldville. General Phillips' Georgia command had literally bled to death in front of the Union entrenchments. More than 600 of his troops had fallen before the enemy works.[100]

Shouts of derision still came from the Union line asking the Southerners if they wanted to come on and try one more time and asking them if they had had enough.

Wounded Confederate General Charles Anderson was informed that Southern troops located to his right were being withdrawn and began withdrawing his 3rd Brigade, Georgia Militia, "slowly and in good order," he would write later in his official report.[101]

Among the soldiers that were slowly extricating themselves from in front of the Union position were the Montgomery County men of Company C, 7th Regiment, Anderson's Brigade. The 19 men that remained slowly withdrew themselves from the mangled battlefield leaving some of their dead.102

Felix Pryor of Mann's 2nd Brigade would write, "...It (fight) ceased about night, when we withdrew, leaving some of our killed and wounded on the field exposed to the severities of a very cold night."

As the Confederates fell slowly back across the 800 yard open field they attempted to bring back as many wounded as they could. In the darkness the wounded were carried, assisted and dragged back towards what was left of Griswoldville.103

When Captain Anderson's Batteries limbered up and pulled back, they had done all that a commander could ask of them. They had not only silenced the Federal guns but assisted the infantry during the advance through the fight and the withdrawal. They had even put the Union commander, General Walcutt, out of the action early on. Captain Anderson's Confederate Battery suffered two killed, one mortally wounded and two others wounded in the fight. General Phillips would say in his report of Captain Anderson and his battery, "He is a skillful, brave, and meritorious officer. The officers and men deported themselves well during the entire action."104

Colonel Catterson sent orders to Major Johnson, 100th Indiana Regiment, Major Willison, 103rd Illinois Regiment, Lt. Colonel Alexander, 46th Ohio Regiment and the other regimental commanders along the mile line to be ready to send skirmishers into the enemy position at the sound of a bugle.105

As the bugle sounded the Union skirmishers left the entrenchments and advanced toward the branch some 50 to 100 yards down the slope. Their orders were, "to bring in such of the enemy as had remained behind in the last repulse and taken shelter under the cover of a ravine which ran along our front." Major Johnson of the 100th Indiana Regiment, would put in his official report.106

As Colonel Catterson's men went out to the fallen rebels, veteran Union Lt. Charles W. Wills, who had seen many battlefields littered with bodies, wasn't prepared for what he saw on this battlefield,

> Old grey haired and weakly looking men and
> little boys, not over 15 years old, lay dead or
> writing in pain. I did pity those boys...I hope we
> never have to shoot at such men again. They
> knew nothing at all about fighting, and I think
> their officers knew as little, or else certainly
> knew nothing about our being there.

The Federals took some of the wounded to the rear and others
they covered with blankets taken from the dead.[107]

Private Theodore Upson was part of the 100th Indiana's
skirmish line that advanced down the hill at dark. Private Upson
would remember,

> We went down on the line where lay the dead
> of the Confederates. It was a terrible sight.
> Some one was groaning. We moved a few
> bodies, and there was a boy with a broken arm
> and leg-just a boy 14 years old; and beside him,
> cold in death, lay his Father, two brothers, and
> an Uncle. It was a harvest of death. We brought
> the poor fellow up to the fire. Our surgeons
> made him as comfortable as they could."[108]

As other Union soldiers walked among the dead, dying and
the wounded Confederates, they tried to assist them.[109]

Further down the line the Northerners found another boy,
whose heart could be seen beating through his torn chest. He
begged for water. "We never wanted to fight," gasped the
wounded Georgia boy.[110]

"There is no God in war," said one Federal soldier who
surveyed the carnage on the battlefield. "It is merciless, cruel,
vindictive, un-Christian, savage, relentless. It is all that devils
could wish for."[111]

Some of the Southern troops had gone into action with their
Negro servants and slaves with them. After the Confederate
retreat back to Griswoldville some had stayed behind in the

covered ravine. Among those captured, Major Willis later noted, were "a number of Africans" in the ravine.[112]

The Georgia Militia, which according to a Missouri Colonel, "once in a while got in our front, and pretended to fight 'just a little,' but they were no real obstacle." Only once, at Griswoldville, Georgia, near Macon, did the militia attempt to check the advance of Sherman's army.[113]

The Federals would use a house owned by a Mr. Baker, two miles from the battlefield, as a hospital for the wounded. The *Macon Telegraph and Confederate* would report in its November 30, 1864 edition,

> Their wounded were quartered there, and
> Mrs. Baker turned out of doors. When the
> Yankee villains left they burned the house,
> giving as a reason for so doing, that it was
> deserted. The entire people throughout the
> section passed over by the enemy, suffered alike.
> They destroyed everything they laid their hands
> on...the railroad between Griswoldville and
> Gordon is completely destroyed. [114]

The screams and moans of the wounded Georgians would echo throughout the cold night.

12 Among Them Are Some of My Best Men and Officers

In the darkness the Federals gathered up the Confederate wounded that they could find, bringing them back into their lines and caring for them around the warm fires throughout the night. They would leave them for their own people to care for in the morning. Some of the wounded the Federals could not find would stay on the battlefield through the freezing night. One soldier of General Sherman's command, serving in the 123rd New York Infantry, Rice Bull, would write of this night in his journal, "The night of the 22nd was very cold, there was a bitter north wind and light snow, however there was plenty of fence rails and much wood had been gathered so we kept warm with rousing fires."₁ Another, a Union Surgeon in the 7th Illinois Regiment, wrote in his diary of the night of November 22, 1864, "...ground frozen- I slept cold..."₂

Sergeant Blanton Nance, Co. E, 7th Regiment, Georgia Militia, was perhaps one of the luckier ones. After receiving painful wounds in the neck and shoulder, he would lay on the field until Union soldiers found him and brought him back to their lines. He was cared for by the Federals until morning.₃

The Union began burying their dead. Private Upson tended to his good friend "Uncle" Wolford whose premonition of his own death had come true. Private Upson would enter this in his diary,

That night after the Johnnys had gone we
buried our dead. We had no coffins, but I could
not bear to think of putting my old friend into his
grave in that way. I remembered that at a house
a short distance away I had seen a gum or hollow
sycamore log of about the length and size. We
got it, split it in halves, put one in the grave dug
in the sandy soil, put his lifeless body in it,
covered it with the other half, filled up the grave
and by the light of a fire we had built with the
rails marked with a piece of lumber pencil his
name, Company, and Regiment.[4]

Major Johnson, 100th Indiana Infantry Regiment, reported his
sending out of the skirmishers, "...resulted in the capture of
several prisoners, most of whom were wounded. We found a
considerable amount of small arms, which I brought in."[5]

Major Willison, 103rd Illinois Regiment, reported his line of
skirmishers, "brought in a few prisoners, besides a number of
wounded. In our front were, by actual count, 51 of the enemy
killed and wounded, 83 stand of small arms were left in our
hands. Our loss was 4 killed and 8 wounded."[6]

The 46th Ohio Regiment, Lt. Colonel Alexander reported,
"There lay in this front about 40 of the enemy's dead and a large
number of wounded.[7]

From some of the Confederate prisoners it was reported that
Brigadier General Phillips had been killed in the action. Union
General Charles Wood's would erroneously report this to
Headquarters First Division, 15th Army Corps, the day following
the battle.[8]

Colonel Robert Catterson, commanding the brigade after
General Walcutt was wounded, sent his report detailing the
capture of 42 prisoners and 150 small-arms. The loss in his
brigade, was listed at 14 killed, 42 wounded and added, "this
list includes only those sent to hospital." Most of Colonel
Catterson's men were pulled from the line at Duncan's farm and
moved on by 9:00 p.m. that night, rejoining their division.[9]

Major Willison commanding the 103rd Illinois Infantry Regiment would report, "At 8 o'clock we received orders to be in readiness to move, and at 9 p.m. moved off the field and rejoined the division." The Northern wounded were loaded into wagons and moved out with the brigade. Only the medical corps stayed longer to assist the Confederate wounded. Fifteen would be brought in and left at a house, not having the transportation to move them.[10]

U. S. Major General O. O. Howard wrote, "We brought along our wounded, (over 200, I believe) in ambulances, jolting over corduroy roads, with much exposure...no loss of life...using rails or newly cut poles, even made our own roads, employing thousands of men." Of the battle in Griswoldville, General Howard would report the next day, "On its complete success in the action yesterday, (November 22) officers from other commands who were looking on say, 'There never was a better brigade of (Federal) soldiers.'"[11]

That night in the Union camps many veteran soldiers remained amazed that the Confederates had dared cross the open field to attack their fortified position. Some Georgians, they agreed, had advanced more than three times against their line. Some of the Southern troops would surge forward seven times trying to break the Union Line. The Yankee's explained the assault as the result of ignorance and inexperience among both the Confederate officers and men. Later, however others wrote admiringly of the Rebels, "dash", "pluck" and "heroic style at the Battle of Griswoldville."[12]

Federal XV Corps commander, Maj. Gen. Peter J. Osterhaus, described the attack in his official report, "Their (the Confederate) columns of infantry marched in heroic style to within fifty yards of our lines. It was all in vain ...When night came the enemy retired, leaving over 300 dead on the battlefield and a number of wounded who were taken care of by our medical corps; also a number of prisoners were taken."[13]

Private Upson of the 100th Indiana Regiment would write in his diary, "...Our Brigade, Wolcutts 2nd of 1st Division 15 A. C. (Army Corps), has been highly commended by General Sherman and all the officers in our Army."[14]

The following night Private Dozer, 26th Illinois Infantry Regiment, would write in ink, "November 23rd Wednesd(ay) Clear & cool. We now had the Macon & Milledgeville RR destroyed. The 2nd & 3rd Brigades were in battle yesterday evening..."[15]

After the fighting General Phillips and his weary men returned to Griswoldville. Mrs. Griswold, who had remained in her home which was one of the few houses not torched by the union troops, would open her three story, twenty room home to the many Confederate wounded. The surgeons were kept busy throughout the night sawing off legs, arms and cutting out bullets. The wounded, one soldier would describe, "...wounded in all possible manner that you can imagine." Among the Confederate wounded were General Anderson, Colonel Mann and Lt. Colonel Evans. The total Southern casualties, which included over sixty other officers, exceeded 600 men.[16, 17]

General Phillips had intended to camp near the village so the remaining wounded and dead could be retrieved from the battlefield, but he soon received orders from Macon,[18]

> The superintendent of the Central railroad will have a train by 9:30 o'clock at the break about two miles and a half this side of Griswoldville. Doctor Rains will accompany the train, and will do all in his power to relieve your wounded men. You will please have your wounded removed to this point with all possible speed. The major-general takes this method of tendering you and the troops of your command his grateful acknowledgments of their gallant conduct in the engagement through which you have passed, and is gratified at your success in driving before you the enemies of your country. Had anything of this character been anticipated, the major-general and staff would have been with you to have shared your danger and your

honor. The reported advance of the enemy from Clinton makes it necessary that you have your command in position in our works at a very early hour to-morrow morning. You will therefore withdraw them as directed in a previous order, after making suitable arrangements for your wounded and giving sufficient time for your men to recover from the fatigue incident to an engagement. The major-general expects information here from the column advancing from Clinton, and if anything of a serious nature occurs he will meet you in person to aid you giving proper directions to your command. Thomas Hardeman Jr. Assistant Adjutant General. [19]

The Confederate wounded that had been left on the battlefield would remain there throughout the freezing night, fighting for their lives. Some would eventually lose that fight, dying alone on the field. "There was mourning in many homes that night for the boys and men who nobly but vainly died that others might be spared. It was madness to fight.... but those boys felt their homes and loved ones were depending upon what they did that day."[20]

Confederate General Phillips' exhausted command would march the final two and half miles in biting cold and wind with the Southern wounded, to the waiting train from Macon. The wounded were carefully loaded into the train by the tired troops. From the Athens Battalion were Lieutenant A. M. Wyng with a severe left arm wound. Pvt. H. U. Durham was helped on the train with a stomach wound. Private J. B. Gardner was helped on with a thigh wound. Private R. W. Bell with a wound to his head was assisted on the train. Lieutenant Milldlebrook, with his knee injury, also boarded. From the Augusta Battalion, Lt. G. P. Weigle with his severe shoulder and side injury would ride back to Macon. Lt. S. Poole wounded in the head would also take the train back.

The train would also take the 3rd Brigade, Georgia Militia,

wounded back with it. From the 8th Regiment, Pvt. J. Hawkins with a severe hip injury and Pvt. C. Tanton with a leg injury would return to Macon on the train. Pvt. William Caswell, the litter bearer wounded while assisting to the wounded on the battlefield would board the train. Capt. Robert Barron, wounded from the Jones County company, would also return to Macon on the train. More than 300 wounded would crowd on the train back to Macon on this cold Georgia night. Many of the almost 600 casualties were either captured, dead or wounded and still lying on the Griswoldville battlefield.21

Captain John J. McArthur's Company C, 7th Regiment, Georgia Militia, helped their wounded board the train. Their wounded including Lt. Gipp Wilcox and Lt. Walter McArthur would be helped on board before they joined the rest of the Georgia troops on the march back to Macon.22

Jonathan Bridges, from the hospital unit, Company C, 11th Regiment, Georgia Militia, would write his wife Fanny, of this most distressing time of his life,

> Camp Cooper, Macon, Georgia
> November 24, 1864
> My Fanny,
> I write you a few lines this morning to let you hear from me. I am not very well at this time. I have a bad cold and am very tired and fatigued. I hope you all may be well and doing well. The Militia has been in a very hard fight and got badly whipped. In my opinion I think that we lost 6 hundred killed and wounded. The fight was at Griswellville 10 miles from Macon. We left Macon in the morning and marched to the fight and fought 3 hours and fell back to Macon the same night. I worked harder than I ever did before in my life lifting wounded men and waiting on them. The hospital was about 1 ½ miles from the battle field and everybody busy. Some cutting off arms and legs and cutting out

bullets. They was wounded in all possible manner that you can imagine. It was the distressingest time I ever say in my life.

There was a good many from our county killed and wounded. I will give you some of the names that I can recall. CAPT. FARWELL, STANELY BRYAN, was killed dead and fell in the hands of the Yankees. RUFUS FLUNINGIN is badly wounded in the hip. COL. NEWSON, ROBERT SHAKELFORD, JAMES JONES, TOM KIDD, MR. COLBEY, CAPT. has slight, WILEY POPE severely and several more. I cannot recollect....[23]

Still other Georgians, after helping their wounded on board, would begin the long nights march back to Macon. Pvt. J. J. Eckles still carrying his home spun blanket, with 27 bullet holes in it, would join his company on the march back to the same city they had left early in the morning. With all the bullet holes that entered his blanket, none would wound him. Pvts. Bridges Smith and W. A. Poe would join the rest of their 5th Georgia Militia on the return march to Macon. Pvt. Bridges Smith would later write of the battle of Griswoldville as being a "fierce encounter".[24]

The train with the wounded would enter Macon much earlier than the 2:00 a.m. arrival the next morning of the exhausted and dispirited Georgia troops who had to march from Griswoldville. Although it was only a 12 mile march, the Georgia troops had fought almost a 4 hour pitched battle, loaded their wounded on the train, then preceded to Macon in the most frigid of conditions. There were concerns among the battered Georgians that night, that after the defeat at Griswoldville, General Sherman might attack Macon.

Felix Pryor of Colonel Mann's 2nd Brigade told of the long walk back to Macon, "...We then marched back near to the ditches and camped on the east side of Macon, the rest of the night about ten miles from the battlefield."[25]

When arriving in Macon the Georgia soldiers would shelter in the cold night in the streets of that city. Some would tear up stair steps and fence rails to keep warm. After several days rest and recuperation in Macon, the Confederate Georgia troops were sent on to Savannah via a safer route. While in Macon they would be reunited with General Carswell's Georgia Militia's, 1st Brigade, now under the command of Colonel Willis, who had been mercifully spared the bloody fighting at Griswoldville.[26]

The Georgia militia soldier, Jack H. King, would write the following day after the Battle of Griswoldville, to his wife Camilla King, anxiously waiting at home. He would tell her of the loss of neighbors and loved ones lost in action.

> Camp Near Fairgrounds
> Macon, 23rd, 1864.
>
> My Dear Darling,
> I wrote you a short note on yesterday, but as the militia has been in a severe engagement I know you will be uneasy about me. Therefore will write you again. The brigades of the militia marched to Griswoldville on yesterday and attacked the yanks in their entrenchments. The loss of our side was severe. General Anderson thinks the casualties in his brigade alone, will amount to 250. Abb Redding poor fellow was killed dead, and fell in the hands of the enemy. A good many were killed and a number of the wounded fell into the hands of the enemies. The fight took place twelve miles from Macon. Our army returned to Macon last night. I would like to give you more information, but can furnish nothing definite, Ben ? was wounded in the face. It is reported that the Yanks have taken Millen and all the forces that were here if that be the case. Mrs. Jenkins and Jim Tharpe have gone ?. From all the information I can get, the yanks are making their way to Charleston and

Savannah, and I can see no way to keep them
from going. My darling Camilla, it is a dark day
for the Southern Confederacy. I have been
suffering from cold. Night before last we
camped in the streets of Macon. All the fire we
could get was by tearing up stair steps so you
can judge what a nice time we had.

Goodby my dearest, Your Jack 27

In the morning, the still tired Georgia troops would be
mustered in the streets of Macon and the ditches of east of
Macon. 1st Sergeant M. C. Adams, Company C, 7th Georgia
Militia from Montgomery County would call the names out.
G. W. Adams, John Adams, M. B. Adams were present for
duty. Thomas Adams was listed as wounded. Groves Conner
was listed as dead. Joe Conner, James Conner, Martin Cauey,
B. Cheny, Littleton Clark, Orien Clark, Andrew Gillis, Elkana
Haralson all would be present for duty. John McArthur was
listed as wounded. Addison McArthur was listed as dead. Allen
McArthur, David Morrison, Daniel Morrison, Duncan McRae
would be listed as present. William Ryals would be listed as
dead. Uriah Sears and C. R. Vaughn would be listed as present
for duty.28
Felix Pryor of the 2nd Brigade, would take pen in hand and
write to his wife Nancy on November 23, from this letter,
although the militia had been smashed at Griswoldville, the
morale remained fairly high. They looked forward to the enemy
attacking their entrenched positions,

...I saw John this morning. He was in the fight
(Griswoldville) and escaped except being a little
stunned by a shell that exploded near him. He
ate dinner with me today. He, like myself, has
been very much fatigued and worn out with
marching, &c. Two of his company were killed
and fifteen wounded on the field. There is some

expectation of an attack in force upon this place. But if they attack us in our breastworks they may not succeed well. I fear the fight yesterday was a badly managed affair, as we lost a good many men and I fear did not gain much for it. I am very uneasy about home as I fear the raiders may have paid us a visit at home. I understand they passed through our county in large force. John says you may make his overcoat as he may need it after awhile. The government has furnished him one suit. My leggings are useful (in) this cold weather. I can't send a letter to you by mail, but write this to you hoping to send it by someone passing home through the country. The Yanks have torn up our railroad badly for some distance below this city, and it seems like we may be cut off from supplies, as we were in Atlanta. Oh, that this cruel war could stop! I desire very much to live at home in peace with you and the dear children. Pray for me and John, that we may escape unharmed and at least return to be with you all to enjoy peace and safety at home. My love to you and all the dear children.   Your affectionate Husband,
                      Felix Pryor[29]

When General Hardee heard about the battle of Griswoldville he would write, "Contrary to my instructions, the militia became engaged in a battle about one mile beyond Griswold and were badly cut up. They lost 51 and 472 wounded, but remained in close contact to the Union army till dark."[30]

Some would blame General Hardee, but too much credit need not be given to Sherman's military genius in tactically deceiving Hardee whose defensive forces were vastly inferior to Sherman's offensive juggernaut. Hardee justifiably felt the need to do the best he could to defend population centers such as Macon, Augusta and Savannah. These necessities would play into the hands of Sherman's army, which marched in four columns through the central Georgia countryside of farms and small towns. [31]

General Taylor would later write, "Joe Brown's army struck the extreme right of Sherman, and suffered some loss before Smith could extricate it...just in time."[32]

Brigadier General Pleasant Phillips would contend that the results could have been different,

> I can but believe if the flank movement had been carried out with all the forces assigned to that duty that it would have resulted in dislodging and probably routing the enemy, notwithstanding he was, I am satisfied, fully equal, if not superior, to our forces. Whiltst we have to regret the loss of many gallant officers and men, yet we cannot but hope that they died not in vain.[33]

General C. D. Anderson in his official report would write, "I am glad to be able say that the men and officers of my command, although they suffered severely, as the list of casualties will show, acted well."[34]

Lieutenant Colonel B. D. Evans would write of his State Line troops in the action,

> Too much commendation cannot be bestowed upon the men of both regiments of the State Line for the handsome manner is which they bore themselves in the charge through the field for a distance of 600 yards under a most destructive fire from the enemy, keeping an unbroken front amidst a hail-storm of bullets, as well as for their determined courage in maintaining their position during the whole engagement. Accompanying herewith I send a list casualties. Among them are some of my best men and officers.

Considering the number engaged, my loss is
heavy.35

General Gustavus Smith's anger was barely concealed in his
official report of the battle of Griswoldville. The action was,
"contrary to my instructions the militia became engaged about
one mile beyond Griswoldville and were badly cut up" and "will
be remembered as an unfortunate accident whose occurrence
might have been avoided by the exercise of proper caution and
circumspection. It in no wise crippled the movements of the
enemy and entailed upon the Confederates a loss, which under
the circumstances could be ill sustained." In his official report
General Smith would also express his appreciation of General
Phillips in "driving before you the enemies of your country."
Unofficially, General Smith remained angry about the slaughter
for the remainder of his life.36

Records would show General Smith brought no action against
General Phillips. He would retain his rank and command in the
Georgia Militia. Soon after the battle General Smith submitted a
"memorandum" for the improvement of the Georgia Militia to
state officials. In the report he brought up the fact there was a
lack of a permanent court-martial militia. He also suggested that
the militia's elected officers, including generals, not be
commissioned until found qualified by a board. Serving officers,
he suggested, should be examined also, and reduced to ranks if
found incompetent.37

One Confederate General wrote of the militia, "The dread the
jeers and sneers they must encounter...more than they do the
bullets of the Yankees." In one account of the battle, by a
Federal historian, he would describe the militia's determined
assault as declaring, "We'll show you that the militia can fight."38

Following the battle of Griswoldville friends and relatives
would travel to Macon to recover their dead and wounded
Georgians. One of those traveling to Macon was John C.
Reynolds, a soldier in the Corps engineers. Upon arriving he
would write to Anna M. Dickey, William Dickey's wife,

Macon Georgia Nov. 28th 1864

Dear Anna,

I got here all safe & sound as I expected on
Saturday evening and hunted William up and
found him at Mr. Flander's quite sick with
Rheumatism & Pneumonia though he is now
improving very rapidly. He was in the fight last
Monday near Griswoldville and was struck on
the hip with a spent ball which though it made
quite a bruise was nothing serious. I have been
as work today & consequently havent had an
opportunity of going to see him but will go again
the first opportunity that I have. Henry Dickey
was in hospital at this place but was transferred
to Geneva on the 24th and was gone before I got
here. I would never have found Wm had it not
been for meeting John Dunbar who is a nurse in
Hospital two. William faring well and I think
will be able to leave in a few days John Mitchell
is with him and I will go to see him every
opportunity I have.

> Truly Your
> Aftn Bro
> Jno. C. Reynolds

NB
Tell Pink to be sure to send me the gloves
Address me in care of Capt. Jno. Glenn
Corps. Engrs
Yrs & c
Jno. C. Reynolds[39]

Union General O. O. Howard would estimate the loss of the
Confederates to be, "...from 1,500 to 2,000 killed, wounded, and
prisoners."[40]

Brigadier-General Charles Woods in his official report of the fight would add, "I cannot speak in too high terms of the coolness and gallantry of Brig. Gen. C. C. Walcutt and Col R. F. Catterson, Ninety-seventh Indiana Infantry. The skill with which they handled the troops and the results obtained show them to be men of marked ability."[41]

On November 27, 1864, General O. O. Howard sent another report to headquarters on the Griswoldville battle,

> The engagement was of a more severe character, and our own loss a little greater than the information led me to suppose, but fortunately the enemy attacked us at the very point where we were prepared, so that with a force only about one-third as large as that of the enemy he was so completely defeated that he has troubled (us) no more in that quarter.[42]

Thomas Osborne, an artillery officer in General Howard's command would write to his two brothers on November 23, 1864, that he had seen the Union casualties from Griswoldville. One man had both legs cut off; another had lost an arm and a leg, and a shell fragment had taken two ounces of flesh from General Walcutt's leg. Osborne believed the healthy marching conditions and clean open air saved many of the wounded.[43]

Rice Bull, 123rd N. Y. Infantry would finish writing of the days events of November 22, in his diary, "...that evening when we arrived, we were notified we were to remain here (Milledgeville) for a days rest. Our right wing had met with some opposition and it would take a day for them to close up and get in line with us."[44]

In his diary Union Surgeon E. P. Burton, Illinois 7th Regiment, would make this entry, "November 24, 1864-Thurs.- Burned all of the houses in Gordon except one-the 2nd Division. Had a sharp little fight with the rebs near here yesterday, repulsed them with great losses." (This must have been at Griswoldville.)[45]

It would take days for news of the battle at Griswoldville to reach the citizens in some parts of Georgia. S. G. Prudden would write to *The Countryman*, a private paper put out by Joseph Addison Turner, a plantation owner in Eatonton, Georgia,

> Mon. 28th-On last Tuesday, there was a battle fought at Griswoldville. Mr. Prudden, in a note of today, gives me the following items: Killed-Dr. J. A. Davis, A.S. Moseley, Paul Wheeler, and J. M. Bonner. Wounded-C. Caswell, mortally; J Middleton, severe, in arm; Ralph Jones, slight, in foot; A. Martin, side; W. Hawkins, severe in hip; H. Baldwin, neck; J. Bowdoin, slight, in foot; W. A. Gatewood, severe, in leg, near thigh.
>
> About eighty were killed, and some four hundred wounded, in the militia...Macon was not attacked.[46]

After the war, Georgia Historian Julius Brown would say, "The statistics show more casualties then any other fight of this war, in proportion to the number engaged."[47]

In the Battle of Griswoldville, although Georgia Militia commanders seldom kept accurate information on troop strength in their reports, it is assumed that they had more than 4,000 men present. The Federal forces with General Walcutt's 1,513 men also adding in the 5th Kentucky and 9th Pennsylvania and the 12th Indiana of Col. Milo Smith's Brigade as well as Captain Arndt's artillerymen. The total Federal force engaged probably numbered 3,000. It is surprising and fortunate for the Confederates that there weren't more killed in action. With over seven-hundred casualties on both sides in the battle there were less than one hundred killed in the battle.

An article in the Athen's *Southern Banner Newspaper* listed the casualties on November 30, 1864.

> Confederate killed and wounded in the Battle of Griswoldville:

2nd Brigade-4th regiment-killed 5; wounded 35; missing 14. 5th regiment-killed 4; wounded 41; wounded mortally 2; missing 3. 6th regiment-killed 4, wounded 39, missing 4. Total Brigade 150.

3rd Brigade-8th regiment- killed 2; wounded 27. 7th regiment-killed 6; wounded 38; missing 8. 9th regiment- killed 17, wounded 51, missing 14. Total Brigade 163.

State Line- killed 3, wounded 40; missing 9. Anderson's Battery- killed 2; mortally wounded 1; wounded 2. Augusta Battalion- killed 1; wounded 23; missing 9. Athens Battalion- killed 3; wounded 40; missing 10. Total State Line 53.

Total aggregate 614.

Federal casualties at Griswoldville were reported to be 14 killed; 79 wounded; 2 missing.[48]

The day after the Battle of Griswoldville excitement would begin to subside in Macon. The *Telegraph and Confederate* Newspaper would report on November 23, 1864,

That a fight occurred today at Griswoldville between the Yankee Cavalry and part of Wheeler's command. The result was highly creditable to our troops.

The enemies infantry is still moving eastward in the direction of Augusta.

The city is remarkable quiet and the people cool and confident.[49]

On November 24 the Macon *Telegraph & Confederate* would publish another article on the Griswoldville battle,

A portion of our forces last night occupied the battle ground of Griswoldville, and the

advance picket line of the enemy was three miles
to the eastward.

The Yankee infantry are still moving in the
direction of Augusta.

Gen. Wheeler yesterday afternoon fought and
drove the enemy from the Railroad a few miles
from Griswoldville, capturing fifty prisoners.

We are glad to state that our authorities relax
none of their vigilance and are perfectly
confident in the ability of our troops to repulse
and attempt the enemy may make against the
city. We think, however, that the Yankee are
satisfied we their experience of that portion of
our forces they encountered at Griswoldville,
and have become satisfied that the road to
Macon is indeed 'hard to travel'.50

On November 26, 1864, the *Telegraph and Confederate*
would try and convince the people that the storm of war had
passed and would run a headline proclaiming,

Macon Is Safe. We are happy to announce
that Macon is considered safe. The commander
of the post has declared the city upon a peace
footing and the order of Major General Cobb,
ordering out every man capable of bearing arms
is withdrawn. This will be pleasing intelligence
to those families whom the emergencies of the
occasion forced from their homes. We trust they
will at once return, and thus escape the many
inconveniences which are the inevitable fate of
the refugee. The city is perfectly quiet and
orderly. We expect, in a few days, everything
will resume its usual appearance. The storm of
war which threatened us has passed. Come
home and bask in the sunlight.51

The Adjutant General of the 1st Brigade of the Georgia
Militia, Col. Thomas Hardeman, who made it back to Macon on
November 22, congratulated Brig. Gen. P. J. Phillips for his
successful stand at Griswoldville. On receiving General Phillips'
report, Col. Hardeman replied, "The Major-General takes this
method of tendering you and the troops of your command his
grateful acknowledgments for their gallant conduct...and is
gratified at your success in driving before you the enemies of
your country..."[52]

Miss Emma Manley would arrive at her home in Spaulding
County on a frigid day riding an oxcart. She found her home
ransacked, the outbuildings burned, and animal carcasses
scattered across the property.[53]

The Georgia Militia was soon on the move from Macon on to
Savannah. Confederate Jonathon Bridges in a letter to his wife
would describe this movement,

> Camp Cooper, Macon, Georgia
> November 24, 1864
> My Fanny,
>   We have marching orders for tomorrow to go
> to Savannah. We will have to go by Albany and
> then to Thomasville and then to Savannah. We
> will have to march about sixty miles afoot. I see
> no prospect of coming home soon. I would like
> to come home by Christmas but I think it
> doubtful. I have not heard from home but once
> in a month. It is very hard to get letters through.
> I am needing some pants very bad and overcoat
> for my pants is nearly gone but I shall not get
> them at all I recon if I go to Savannah. I put on
> clean shirt and drawers this morning for the
> reason the lice was about to eat me up. I killed
> fifty yesterday off my shirt. I have been nearly
> frozen for two days. Night before last I never
> slept one wink. I was lifting wounded men all
> night long. I have not heard from JOHN in some

time and would like to hear from him. I am
faring very well except some clothing. I am not
in danger of the bullets much and have tents to
sleep under. I will write you a letter again soon
if I can. You must write to me direct as before
until I inform you different.

Your Jonathan as ever.[54]

General P. G. T. Beauregard would later give five reasons
why he didn't countermand General Hood's campaign into
Tennessee instead of pursuing General Sherman's army through
Georgia. The fifth reason read as follows from his report,

From the assurances of Governor Brown and
Major-General Cobb, it was a reasonable
supposition that about 17,000 men would be
furnished in a great emergency by the state of
Georgia, which force, added to thirteen brigades
of cavalry, under Major-General Wheeler, and
some 5,000 men, who, it was thought, might be
drawn from the States of North and South
Carolina, would have given us about 29,000 men
to throw across Sherman's path.[55]

General Beauregard never mentioned in his memo how a
force of 29,000 men, made up mainly of militia, workshop and
State reserve troops, would be able to stop or even impede
Sherman's army, when Hood's veteran battle-harden army hadn't
had any luck with this same force just months before.

A poem published in the Macon *Telegraph and News* during
the war,

Farewell, each noble Georgian son,
Our hearts for you still sigh-
While freedom's triumph shall be won,
Your names shall never die. [56]

13   Epilogue

Southern Historians would later write of the battle of
Griswoldville as "....a battle fought for the salvation of the
commercial metropolis of this State-an engagement won almost
exclusively by Georgians-a victory which, in the results achieved,
may be justly esteemed as decisive, and pregnant with honor to
Confederate arms."[1]

Union General Walcutt would survive the battle and would
reach Savannah with Sherman's army, traveling by carriage.

Union Colonel Robert Catterson would command the 2nd
Brigade through most of the campaign in Georgia and the
Carolinas. He would become one of the last brigadier generals of
the Civil War. The Indiana native would survive the war and die
in a veterans hospital in San Antonio, Texas.[2]

Union Pvt. Theodore Upson, 100th Indiana Regiment, would
survive the war and march with the 100th Indiana in Washington
in the Victory Parade of May 20, 1865. He would keep his
promise to his good friend "Uncle" Aaron Wolford. He took his
friends testament, watch, and money and sent them to Wolford's
wife back home in Indiana. Upson would burst into tears when
he tried to describe Uncle Aaron's burial, and moved away from
his companions to finish the letter, "I am afraid she will have
hard work to read it, for I could not help blotting the paper."
Upson hoped that his friends wife and eight children would,
"...realize what a grand soul he had." He was 20 years old when
the war ended. His letters of the war would later be published
into a book titled, *With Sherman to the Sea*. He died in 1919 at
the age of 74.[3]

Private Jesse L. Dozer of the 26th Illinois Infantry would
survive the March to the Sea with Sherman and would make his

last entry in his daily dairy on April 29, 1865, "Saturday Cloudy & warm. We started from Raleigh where we were camped about 3 weeks from Richmond Va dis of 175 miles on our way to Washington city..."[4]

Confederate Sergeant Blanton Nance, Co. E, 7th Regiment, survived his two wounds at Griswoldville. Wounds that would disable him for many months. After the war he resided in Macon, Georgia, where he served seven or eight years as captain of police. He lived a long life before dying at his home in Macon.[5]

Confederate Private W. A. Poe, 5th Regiment, would survive the battle of Griswoldville to reach his 15th birthday on December the second, 1864. He would also live to see the wars end. He would die in the city he fought to defend, Macon, on June 19, 1919[6]

Thirteen year old Private Bridges Smith, 5th Regiment, Georgia Militia, would survive the war to become Mayor of Macon, Georgia, the same city where he had worked in the munitions factory during the war. He would die on October 5, 1930.[7]

Private William Caswell, litter bearer of Company H, 5th Regiment, Georgia Militia wounded in the back at Griswoldville would be reported to have suffered a wound to the back in the Macon *Telegraph and Confederate* newspaper. A retraction would be sent to the paper by his company commander Captain Adams. It read,

> Please allow me to make a correction in relation to Wm. C. Caswell, of Company H 5th regiment, as reported by me in your paper of this morning. Mr. Caswell was wounded dangerously thru the hips, (instead of the back as I reported) whilst gallantly discharging his duty on the field as a littler bearer. I make this correction in justice to a gallant soldier, as some persons think it discreditable to be wounded in the back.[8]

Major Ferdinand Cook, commander of the Athens Battalion, survived the battle but would not be returning to the Athens Armory. He died in action less than three weeks later with his command at a battle near Hardeeville, South Carolina on December 11, 1864.[9]

Mr Griswold founder of Griswoldville would never rebuild his factories. He lost three quarters of a million dollars with its destruction. He sold his land and other possessions. He died September 1867, and was buried at Clinton, Georgia.[10]

Church records would show that the Mountain Springs Baptist Church would hold no meetings on November 26 and 27, 1864. "No meetings or conference held on account of Yankee raids." There would be no record of meetings for four months.[11]

The town named after Mr. Griswold, Griswoldville, would never be rebuilt. In 1900 a census would report 79 inhabitants would still call Griswoldville home. It also added that the town still boasted a money order post office and some good stores. It would eventually die along with the old south. If you look for it on a road map of Georgia, you won't find it listed. If you passed by in an automobile you would hardly know that a town once existed in that location.

In 1996, this article appeared in *Blue & Gray* magazine,

> Fought ten miles east of Macon, Georgia, the Battle of Griswoldville was the only engagement fought by Maj. Gen. William T. Sherman's army during his "March to the Sea." The battle occurred November 22, 1864, when a division of Georgia militia under P. J. Phillips ignored orders not to engage the enemy, and attacked a strong Federal defensive position around the Duncan Farm. Phillips' militia, comprised largely of young boys and elderly men, suffered heavy losses.
>
> The Association for the Preservation of Civil War Sites' acquisition of 18.5 acres of the

Griswoldville battlefield was made possible by a
generous donation of $23,000 by David Cason, a
retired teacher. Alerted to preservation efforts at
Griswoldville through the APCWS newsletter,
Cason made the donation in memory of his
parents. APCWS plans to construct an
interpretive trail on the battlefield, with wayside
exhibits and parking.[12]

After the battle of Griswoldville the militia and other state
units would get the recognition they had so desired. In the
Augusta *Daily Constitutional* newspaper dated November 30,
1864. "The militia fought like veteran soldiers. Major Cook in
command of the Augusta and Athens Battalions, we learn, acted
most gallantly." From the Athens *Southern Banner* newspaper
dated November 30, 1864. "Hereafter there will be no jeers at
the militia. Their gallant conduct in the battle of Griswoldville
has elicited the respect and admiration of all" and "These troops
as well as the militia forces, acted like veterans and faced the
destructive enemy fire with as much firmness as could have been
displayed by the heroes of Hood or Lee."[13]

General Gustavus Smith and his command then received a
commendation for their conduct and services on March 9, 1865,
from the Georgia Legislature. [14]

Resolved, by the Senate and House of
Representatives, in General Assembly met, that
the thanks of the State are due and are hereby
tendered to General G. W. Smith, and to the
officers and men composing the First Division of
Georgia militia, and to the officers and men of
the Georgia State Line, for their conspicuous
gallantry at Griswoldville in this State; and
especially for their unselfish patriotism in
leaving their State and meeting the enemy on the
memorable and well fought battlefield at Honey
Hill in South Carolina.

> The State with pride records this gallant
> conduct of her militia, and feels assured that
> when an emergency again arises State lines will
> be forgotten by her militia, and a patriotism
> exhibited which knows nothing but our whole
> country.[15]

The militia was sent on to Grahamville and Coosawhatchie. The militia was needed in South Carolina but wasn't suppose to leave Georgia boundaries. General Smith personally asked the troops if they would go with him into South Carolina where they were needed. All agreed to join Smith in his foray into South Carolina. At the battle of Honey Hill, November 30, 1864, the entrenched militia, along with other Georgia units totaling 1,400 men defeated a Union force three times its size. The Confederates suffered 50 casualties, the Federals 754. The 1st Brigade Georgia Militia, Georgia State Line, Augusta Battalion and the Athens Battalion participated in the action. The Battle of Honey Hill came only eight days after the Battle of Griswoldville. Could the "inexperienced" officers and men of the militia have learned that much about fighting in eight days to fight and win against a numerically stronger force. Or as General Longstreet knew and General Hood would soon find out at Franklin, Tennessee, that infantrymen can't frontally attack a well entrenched force without suffering horrendous losses. General G. W. Smith would die June 24, 1896.[16]

Brigadier-General C. D. Anderson died on February 23, 1901.

Brigadier-General Henry K. McCay died July 30, 1886.

Private Henry Mercer, from Wilkinson County, one of the first wounded in the battle would survive the action and live a long life in Georgia.[17]

Emma Manley would survive the war and live out her life in Griffin, Georgia. Emma would say she had received letters from the kind Union General Spencer after the war had ended. In Mary's opinion, the general "was smitten." Emma would say, "Had I remained at my home in Spalding County, I would not have seen a single Yankee."[18]

Brigadier-General P. J. Phillips would go to his grave believing he had met a full Union division on that cold November day in Griswoldville, Georgia. Had Phillips been drinking the morning of the battle as some of his soldiers insisted? Would it have been fought any differently if he had been drinking or not? General Phillips died on October 12, 1876.

Governor Joe Brown in his message to Georgia of February 17, 1865, would write,

> ...For eight months the Confederate reserves, officers, civil as well as military, had kept the field almost constantly, participating in every important fight from Kenesaw to Honey Hill. If the sons of Georgia under arms in other States had been permitted to meet the foe upon her own soil, without assistance, General Sherman's army could never have passed from the mountains to the seaboard.
>
> In conclusion, Governor Brown claimed that Georgia during the fall and winter had a larger proportion of her white male population under arms than any other state in the Confederacy.

The Confederate Monument in Griffin, Georgia reads:
"Our tribute of gratitude, reverence and love to the soldiers of the Confederate States Of America."

Years later a farmer, Mr. Harvie Birdsong, plowing around the remnants of the large pine in the center of the battlefield, on the old Duncan farm, had his plow catch under one of its roots. He looked down and saw a minnie ball mixed in with the dirt. Rooting around in the rotted sap that had collected around the base of the tree, he found countless others. Long ago mementoes of the Griswoldville battle. A time when the tree shared this ground with fields of gray. [19]

The order of Battle at Griswoldville was as follows:

FEDERAL FORCES ENGAGED

SECOND BRIGADE, FIRST DIVISION
XV ARMY CORPS

Brigadier General Charles C. Walcutt (Wounded)

Colonel Robert F. Catterson

97th Indiana Infantry Regiment
Colonel Robert F. Catterson
Captain George Elliott

103rd Illinois Infantry Regiment
Major Asias Willison

6th Iowa Infantry Regiment
Major William H. Clune

40th Illinois Infantry Regiment
Lt. Colonel Hiram W. Hall

100th Indiana Infantry Regiment
Major Ruel M. Johnson

46th Ohio Infantry Regiment
Lt. Colonel Isaac N. Alexander

5th Kentucky Cavalry Regiment (Kilpatrick)
Colonel Oliver L. Baldwin

5th Kentucky Cavalry Regiment (Kilpatrick)
Colonel Oliver L. Baldwin

9th Pennsylvania Cavalry Regiment (Kilpatrick)
Colonel Thomas J. Jordan

12th Indiana Infantry Regiment (Milo Smith's Brigade)
Major Elbert D. Baldwin

1st Michigan Artillery, Battery B
Captain Albert Arndt
(2-3 inch Rodman guns)

CONFEDERATE FORCES ENGAGED

FIRST DIVISION GEORGIA MILITIA
Brigadier General Pleasant J. Philips

SECOND BRIGADE GEORGIA MILITIA
Colonel James N. Mann
4th, 5th and 6th Regiments

THIRD BRIGADE GEORGIA MILITIA
Brigadier General Charles D. Anderson
7th Regiment - Colonel Abner Redding
8th Regiment - Colonel William B. Scott
9th Regiment - Colonel J. M. Hill

FOURTH BRIGADE GEORGIA MILITIA
Brigadier General Henry K. McCay
10th Militia Regiment
11th Regiment - Colonel William T. Toole
12th Regiment - Colonel Richard Sims

GEORGIA STATE LINE (1st & 2nd Regiments)
Lt. Colonel Beverly D. Evans (Wounded)
Lt. Colonel James Wilson

ATHENS LOCAL DEFENSE BATTALION
Major Ferdinand W.C. Cook

AUGUSTA LOCAL DEFENSE BATTALION
Major George T. Jackson

Anderson's Light Artillery Battery
Captain Ruel W. Anderson
(4 - 12 Pounder Napoleons)

TOURING THE BATTLEFIELD

The Griswoldville battlefield is approximately 10 miles east of Macon, Georgia and may be reached by taking U.S. Highway 80 East from the city. After crossing the Ocmulgee River, proceed another two and a half miles and take the left fork onto Georgia Highway 57. Follow Highway 57 approximately three and a half miles and take the unmarked paved road to your left, proceeding northward another mile and a quarter to the railroad, the site of old Griswoldville. The site is now completely abandoned but the railroad still follows the original roadbed and just across the tracks on your right is the pond which fed the war time grist and saw mills.

Cross the railroad and turn immediately to the right on the dirt road running parallel to the tracks. Proceed four tenths of a mile and cross over the railroad to your right and continue another six tenths of a mile to Georgia Historical commission marker on the left entitled, BATTLE OF GRISWOLDVILLE, THE DEPLOYMENT AND ASSAULTS. Continue another three tenths of a mile to a marker on your left entitled, THE CAVALRY SKIRMISH.

On the western edge of the battlefield there are two more markers. Originally there were some ten historic markers adorning the now deserted town and battlefield.

Proceed another three tenths of a mile, turn left and continue another four tenths of a mile across Battle Line Branch to the crest of the hill. You will be at the approximate center of Brigadier General Charles C. Walcutt's Federal line and will have approached the crest of the hill on the same approximate axis as the main Confederate attack. Walcutt's line ran approximately six tenths of a mile northward and to your left to the railroad and approximately four tenth of a mile southward and to your right to the Big Sandy Swamp.

About 40 unmarked Union graves can be located near the

Mountain Springs Baptist Church.

Federal dead from not only the Griswoldville battle, but cavalry actions that took place near the area, between Kirkpatrick's and Wheelers's troopers. To travel to the old Battle Graveyard follow U. S. Highway 80, east from Macon, Georgia for five miles, then take Georgia No. 57 for three miles. There at a State Historic Griswold marker and the new brick Mountain Springs Church on left of highway, turn left two miles on dirt highway and you are there. Unmarked Confederate graves can be found near the swamp, on the southern part of the battlefield, near the left of the Union line. These are some of the dead from the battle of Griswoldville. Other Confederates were taken back to Macon and buried in the historic Rose Hill Cemetery.

Georgia Historical Markers located on the Griswoldville Battlefield site.

BATTLE OF GRISWOLDVILLE

On November 22, 1864, the Right Wing (15th and 17th Corps) of Gen. Sherman's army (U) moved SE from Clinton (near Gray) toward Gordon and Irwinton on its destructive March to the Sea. Walcutt's brigade, with two guns of Arndt's Michigan Battery, was posted on the right to protect the movement from the persistent harassment of Wheeler's cavalry © from the direction of Macon.

Near Griswoldville (4 miles E), Walcutt was attacked by a division of Georgia Militia © under Brig. Gen. P. J. Phillips who approached via this road. After three hours of fighting in which both sides suffered severely, Phillips was forced to withdraw. (Ga 49 at the Bibb County Line.)

THE CAVALRY SKIRMISH

On the night of November 21, 1864, Murray's brigade of Kilpatrick's cavalry (U), which during the day had burned buildings and destroyed railway facilities in Griswoldville, camped on the E fork of Little Sandy Creek, 1 ½ miles NE. At dawn, Murray's pickets were driven in by Wheeler's cavalry (C), which was met by the 9th Pennsylvania and 5th Kentucky cavalry. Fighting developed in the fields to the NE until mid-morning when Walcutt's brigade (U) arrived, enabling Murray to drive Wheeler through Griswoldville and reoccupy the town. About noon, they were forced to retire by the advance of the 1st Division, Georgia Militia, from Macon.
(Southeast of Griswold at the County Line, near J.L. Stribling's home.)

BATTLE OF GRISWOLDVILLE

On November 22, 1864, the Right Wing (15th and 17th Corps) of Gen. Sherman's army (U) marched southeast from the vicinity of Gray toward Gordon and Irwinton on its destructive March to the Sea. To protect the right against Wheeler's cavalry (C), Brig. Gen. C.C. Walcutt's brigade of Woods' division, 15th Corps, with two guns of Arndt's Michigan Battery, was sent toward Macon. Near Griswoldville, Walcutt found Murray's brigade of Kilpatrick's cavalry division engaged with Wheeler. Together, they drove Wheeler through Griswoldville, after which Walcutt withdrew and took up a strong position on the Duncan farm, south of the railroad and about 1 ½ miles east of town. He intrenched hastily on a slight elevation behind a small stream (Little Sandy Creek), his flanks protected by swamps and open fields in his front. The guns were placed on the road near the center of his line.

About 2:30 p.m. he was attacked by 1st Division, Georgia Militia, Brig. Gen. P. J. Phillips, with four guns. Advancing in three lines across the open fields, the Georgia's made seven determined assaults; they silenced Arndt's guns but could not break the Union line. About 3:30 p.m., Walcutt was wounded and Col. R. F. Catterson, 97th Indiana Infantry, assumed command.

At dusk, Phillips was forced to retire but Catterson made no attempt to pursue him. Killed and wounded: © 532; (U) 92. (Ga 18 in Griswoldville.)

THE BATTLE OF GRISWOLDVILLE
THE ADVANCE FROM EAST MACON
On November 22, 1864, the 1st Division, Georgia Militia (less the 1st Brigade), with the 1st and 2nd Regiments, Georgia State Line, and Anderson's Georgia State Line, and Anderson's Georgia Battery attached, Brig. Gen. Pleasant J. Phillips commanding, marched from east Macon about 8:00 a.m. en route to Augusta. About a mile west of Griswoldville, Phillips found the Athens and Augusta local defense battalions, under Maj. F. W. C. Cook, formed in line of battle facing the town, through which elements of Wheeler's cavalry © had just been driven by Walcutt's brigade of Woods' division, 15th Corps, and Murray's brigade of Kilpatrick's cavalry division (U).

Forming line of battle with Anderson's brigade on the right, the Athens and Augusta battalions in the center, McCoy's brigade on the left, Mann's brigade in reserve and the State Line regiments deployed as skirmishers in his front, Phillips advanced to Griswoldville, only to find that the enemy had retired.

Unaware that Walcutt had halted and intrenched about 1 ½ miles east, south of the railroad, to protect the right of Sherman's army then moving on the Irwinton road, Phillips reassembled his command and began moving it east of town to await further orders. (In Griswoldville)

BATTLE OF GRISWOLDVILLE
THE DEPLOYMENT AND ASSAULTS

About 1:30 p.m., November 22, 1864, after halting in Griswoldville to reform his column and report his progress, Brig. Gen. P. J. Phillips began moving his command (1st Division, Georgia Militia and attached units) east to clear the town, intending to halt there and await further orders. When the head of the column reached this vicinity, firing was heard about on half mile to the front. Riding forward, Phillips found Cook's Athens and Augusta battalions engaged with Walcutt's brigade (U) which, after retiring from Griswoldville, had taken up a strong position behind Little Sandy Creek, about one half mile east.

Sending Cook to the right, Phillips deployed Evans' State Line regiments on his left with McCoy's brigade on Evans' left, its left near the railroad, Anderson's brigade formed north of the railroad, its left parallel with the tracks. Anderson's battery was posted on the railroad. About 2:30 p.m., Phillips advanced in three lines across the open fields southeast of this point.

Although he made seven assaults on the intrenched Union line his untrained militia could not dislodge Walcutt's battle-wise veterans and he was finally forced to retire toward Macon. (Near the railroad one mile east of Griswoldville)

Special Correspondence of the Constitutionalist
FROM THE FRONT.

Battle of Griswoldville—Sherman's course and forces—Depredations of the enemy—Occupation of Sandersville—Conway's men—A gallant scout.

SPARTA, Nov. 27th, 9 P. M.

Mr. Editor: We have information from men belonging to Furgoson's division of cavalry of the fight at Griswoldville on Tuesday. A feint was made on Macon on Sunday afternoon by some of Kilpatrick's cavalry, but Wheeler's forces were put in line of battle up and down Walnut creek, and after some heavy skirmish-ing, the enemy fell back to Griswoldville, where he constructed breastworks of fence rails. On Tuesday Wheeler attacked them again, but fail-ed to drive them until our infantry came up (composed mainly of militia.) The enemy gave way, and we followed them about three miles.—Our loss was about four hundred in killed, wound-ed and missing. The enemy's much heavier.—Our informant, who was in the fight, says we took two hundred and fifty prisoners in one batch, and others were taken, he knows not how many. The enemy fell back towards Gordon and Milledgeville, and destroyed the road as he went. A man who was taken prisoner while helping to repair the road, on Wednesday, says he counted fifty-one dead Confederates on the field, among whom was the brave Col. Redding, of the militia. The Yankees, as usual, tried to claim the victory.

188

The Engagement at Griswoldville.

We learn from the *Macon Telegraph*, by private letters, and from Capt. Hill, who participated in the fight, that a battle was fought at Griswoldville, on the Central railroad, on Tuesday of last week.

We copy the following from the *Telegraph & Confederate*. It will be seen that Maj. Cook and our boys fought gallantly.

"On Tuesday afternoon our forces under command of General Philips came upon the pickets of the enemy this side of Griswoldville. Our forces immediately deployed in line of battle and skirmishers were thrown forward. They drove in the pickets and then advancing upon their skirmish line, drove them steadily backwards through the town and two miles beyond, where they came upon the main body of the enemy strongly entrenched. Our men advanced boldly to the attack and a severe and protracted fight continued until dark, when our troops were ordered to fall back, which they did in the best of order. No attempt was made by the enemy to follow.

We learn that the militia force behaved with distinguished gallantry, advancing upon the enemy's breastworks in perfect order and with no straggling. They charged through an open field to within fifty yards of the Yankee works and maintained their ground till ordered to withdraw.

The Athens Battalion, commanded by Maj. Cook, and the Augusta Battalion, under Maj. Jackson, both under the immediate orders of the former officer, were distinguished for the cool and steady manner in which they bore themselves in the battle. These troops, as well as the militia forces, acted like veterans, and faced the destructive fire of the enemy with as much firmness as could have been displayed by the heroes of Hood or Lee.

We have heard no estimate of the enemy's loss.—*Telegraph & Confederate, November 24.*

Battle of Griswoldville.

Sergeant Weigle, of Co. A, Augusta Battalion, left Macon on Thursday last, furnishes us with the following particulars of the battle of Griswoldville.

He states that three Brigades of militia, two regiments of State line troops, the Athens and Augusta Battalions, all under the command of Gen. Phillips, engaged the enemy on Tuesday November 22d. He first attacked them at Griswoldwille about 12 o'clock. The enemy fell back one mile on the Central railroad, towards Savannah, where they had erected three lines of fortifications.

Gen. Philips pursued them to their breastworks, when he ordered a charge, driving the enemy from his first line of defenses. The enemy made several desperate efforts to recapture the works, but were repulsed each time with heavy loss. Gen. Philips held his position during the night. The enemy had withdrawn next morning.

Our forces in charging the enemies breastworks through an open field were exposed to a galling fire in which they lost heavily, between 350 and 400 killed and wounded; as an evidence of the storm of leaden hail they passthrough, the colors of the Augusta Battalion bears the mark of *sixteen* federal bullets.

The militia fought like veteran soldiers.
Maj. Cook in command of the Augusta and
Athens Battalions, we learn, acted most gal-
lantly.

Sergeant Weigle, of Company A, Augusta
Battalion, furnishes us with the following list of
casualties in the Athens Battalion, commanded
by Maj. F. W. C. Cook:

Casualties in Athens Battalion at Griswoldville, Nov. 22d, 1864, Maj. F. W. C. Cook, commanding:

CO. A, CAPT. SIMS, COMMANDING.

Wounded—Lieut A M Wyng, left arm, severe;
Lieut A P Hans, head, slight; Privates J M
Glon, hand; J A Moody, hand; R W Bell, head.
Missing—Wm Parke.

CO. B, LIEUT. MAINUS COMMANDING.

Killed—Lieut J H Hunter, C Clearland.
Wounded—Lieut Mainus slight, Sergt T C War-
ner, Jas Brack, Jas Beardon, Thomas Bible slight,
M R Baggs arm, severe; Jas Brane mouth, J H
Dudson hand, H U Durham stomach, Jas Few
foot, Gellart struck by shell, J B Gardner thigh,
M A Millsass both thighs, J L Miller struck by
shell, T McArdle in head, J Middlebrooks struck
by shell, B W Waters slight, J W White struck
by shell, S M White through both thigh, W J
Wallace in foot. R H Hernad mortally.

CO. C.—CAPT. PENDEGRASS COM'D'G.

Wounded—Capt Pendegrass, Sergt Framer,
Corp'l Booth, Alex Hamuth, D Hodges, A Mass,
N H Rhodes, Wm Stone, John Wright, Wm
Walker.
Missing—S M Bassett, J H Beall, R Beall, J
R Cawthres, A D Snow, O Stone, W R Tanny.

CO. D—CAPT. ELLIOTT COM'D'G.

Killed—John Chancy.
Wounded—Lieut Middlebrooks, knee; D
Richardson, hand, slight; W C Hall, breast,
slight; T G Jordan, arm, slight.
Missing—M G Durham, Jack Fleeman.

CAMP NEAR MACON, GA.,
November 23d, 1864.

Casualties in the Augusta Battalion, November 22d, at Griswoldville, Maj. Geo. T. Jackson commanding :

CO. A—CAPT. T. H. HOLLEYMAN COM'D'G.

Wounded—Lieut T A H Meyer, hand, slight; W O Dunbar, arm, severe; R J Morrison, leg, slight; Simeon Buford, arm, severe; John Copeland, foot, slight; Wm Churchill, shoulder, slight.

CO. B, CAPT. JACOB ADAM, COMMANDING.

Wounded—Capt Adams, slightly; Lieut G P Weigle, severely in shoulder and side; private Goodyear, severely in shoulder.
Missing—Corp'l Job.

CO. C, CAPT. A. T. SMITH, COMMANDING.

Lieut S Poole, seriously in head; Serg't W H Murden, in thigh, severe; D Gaunt, seriously in shoulder; K Lublin, dangerously in head and thigh; W O Cartwright, in leg; J D Andrews, slightly in shoulder; W H Woods, in head slight; Jerry Gleason, slight in leg.
Missing—Geo Shiver, Jas Walker, M P Scales, John Scales.

CO D, LIEUT JAS. C. SEXTELL, COMMANDING.

Killed—A Belcher.
Wounded—Corp'l Welch, slight in leg; H Frydell, leg and arm; D Haslop, slight in neck; Joe Hudson, slight in arm; J Lemore, slight in hand; Jas Hearing, slight in hip.

CO. E, LIEUT. SHACKLEFORD, COMMANDING.

Missing—Lieut Shackleford.
Wounded—Geo Tomens, slight; Henry Reeves, slight.

JAS. T. GARDINER,
Adj't Augusta Batt.

192

List of casualties of the Third Brigade C. M., in the battle near Griswoldville, on the 22nd Nov., 1861, General C. D. Anderson Commanding.

The General received two bullets through his clothes and was badly wounded in the hand.— Captain Adams, of the staff, slightly wounded. Lieut. Hamilton, of the staff, slightly wounded.

SEVENTH REGT., COL. A. F. REDDING commd.

Col. A F Redding killed.

Co A, Lieut Sikes Commanding.

Slightly Wounded: W Sikes, in leg; Sergt Thomas Dumas, in arm; Private Wm Evans, in foot. Missing: Private Wm Banks.

Co F, Capt R G Fulgam Commanding.

Wounded: Capt Fulgam, in leg; Sergt D H Henley, in thigh and leg, seriously; John L Anderson, in thigh, seriously; John King, in thigh, slightly. Wounded and Missing: Lt A G McPhail.

Co D, Lt A G Green, Commanding.

Killed: Corpl T G King. Slightly Wounded: Jas White, in foot; Obadiah Edge, in ankle; T H Cook, in arm.

Co H, Capt C C Hightower, Commanding.

Killed: Sergt George A Gardner. Slightly Wounded: Capt C C Hightower, in foot; Jack Bussey, in shoulder; James Coppage, in thigh.

Co[ ], Capt D F McRae, Commanding.
Killed : J C McLean : Wounded : [ ] F
McRae, in arm ; Lt Powell, in ankle ; Lt L
McDuffee, in shoulder ; Corpl Dubs McRae,
in hand ; Sgt Wm F Williams, in breast ; Mis-
sing : D D Lomhady.

Co D, Capt S D Fuller, commanding.
Wounded : R A Gibbs, in shoulder ; Allen
Marshall, in thigh. Wounded and Missing : G
W Young, J A Gibbs and Darling Grain.

Co C, Lt Lewis Wilcox, commanding.
Killed : Gibbs, Conner. Wounded : Lt W
Wilcox, in thigh ; Sergt J W McArthur, in
side ; Sgt Wm R Ryals, in knee ; Thos B Al-
tmas, in hand ; W D Penick, in foot ; Kiah
Wilcox, severely and supposed killed. Missing :
A C McArthur.

Co [ ], Capt W T Morgan, commanding.
Wounded : Capt W T Morgan, slightly ;
Capt S H Singleton, severely in head ; Arthur
Newton, slight head ; —— Horton, slight
leg. Missing : E Erwin, H Johnson, Sergt B
Nance, D Ward, Wm Warren.

Co B, Capt J P Collier, commanding.
Wounded : Corpl A Collard, foot slightly ;
Corpl J A G Pilinazee, breast, sli ; J T Chilb,
foot ; R Whatley, thigh, sev ; John Winn, missing.

EIGHTH REGIMENT, COL. W. B. SCOTT COM'D'G.

Co A, Lt B F White, Commanding.

Wounded: Lt B F White, both knees; W F Craswell, both lungs; Jas Bryant, slt; Jas Ery, O T Myneh, shoulder, (missing.)

Co B, (in detached service.)

Co C, Lt M Jones, Commanding.

Wounded: Sergt B F Fenney, jaw; C Taunton, through leg, slt.

Co D, Capt E Cumming, Commanding.

Wounded: Lt E Adkins, mortally; J R Smith, through left side; A Ogburn, body and leg; Lt P H Rawle, thigh, slt; Andrew Chandlers, through thigh, d sh; W L Smith, hand, slt

Co E, Sgt Beckom Commanding.

Killed: Elias Champion. Wounded: J D Tharp, arm

Co F, Lt G W Thames Commanding.

Wounded: S F Bryant, slt

Co G, Lt ——— Holloman, Commanding.

Wounded: Corpl W R Gilbert, both thighs; J Harris, leg; M Dominac, arms; A Vinson, through leg and missing.

Co H, Capt R H Barrow Commanding.

Killed: W H Jolly. Wounded: Lt John Baker, wrist, sev; N Morris, right arm; Jho Humphries, through left hand; Wiley Vinson side, slt.

Co K, Capt T M Hunt, Commanding.

Wounded: W D Daring, side and arm; J Hawkins, hip, sev; J Vanzint, both knees, slt; W Cairy, hand, sev.

M. D. BOATWRIGHT,
Adit. 8th Regt., 3d Brigade.

N. P. Cartwright,
Adjt. 8th Regt., 3d Brigade.

NINTH REG'T, COL. B. M. HILL, COM'G.

Lt Col T. S Sherman, slight in shoulder ; Maj W A Turner, slight in leg.

Co A. Killed : J C Forbes, A W Phillips. Wounded : L Shell, thigh ; X T Crawford, thigh ; S L Lester, left arm ; R D Smith, elbow. Missing : John Deaker.

Co B. Killed : Jas Callaway. Wounded : Corpl W T Bassey, both feet and arms ; John P Oeain, shoulder, slight ; Thos Hattawn, mortally, since dead ; John B Pope, slight in shoulder ; P Strozier, slight in hip and shoulder ; L M Chunn, slight in shoulder.

Co C. Wounded : J W Hammock, hand and head ; Lt J B Chambliss, severe in foot ; Sgt R M Canton, slight in arm ; W Rotherme, mortally in body ; H M Smith, mortally and missing. Missing : H M Snead and A Teal.

Co D. Killed : Lt L Farmer. Wounded : Lt Simms, mortally ; Lt S Kint, slightly ; 1st Lt Lee, in hip ; Corpl Dykes, slightly ; Dr J S Henry, slight in leg ; John Anderson, slight ; Ira Scroggins, severely.

Co E. Killed : Capt E F Strozier. Wounded : Sgt Thomas Mitcham, severe in arm ; W D Mathews, severely in thigh ; M C W Stewart, slight.

Co F. Killed : Lt J W Spires, H T Butts — Wounded : Lt R F Patillo, slightly ; B G McKenney, slightly ; G W Childs, thigh broke ;

W I Cole, mortally ; C L Green, slightly.

Co F, Sergt R B Lyle, Corpl H M Jackson, T A Dallas, missing.

Co G, M A Harris, B V R Boddie killed ; J R Copeland mortally wounded ; W S Saxon, George Cook, Jno H Hubbard, David Evins slightly wounded ; C M Grant severe ; J Freeman, J Blow, C ● Grant, C William missing.

Co H, Sgt A N Camp killed ; Capt B ___ Lt J D Thurman, Sgt J B L Watson, Co __ Rall, J W Odom, J W Moore, slightly wounded ; J R Cotton severely.

Co I, J W Davidson, J A Clenis ___ Wilson Hargett, wounded mortally ; Dillia- mer, severely, in wrist ; J A Hullis slight.

in leg ; J R McDaniel, slight ; ___ Thett, now, slight ; J A Goodman and ___ Buch missing.

Co K, Capt W O Winborn, slight in leg and thigh ; Lt Jac T Phillips, ___ hand ; S Beckey, severely in thigh ; T ___ berry, slight in leg ; J H Willis, seven shoulder and arm, slight in hand ; J B ___ tor, slightly in knee and both arms ; Sgt __ Leonard, H C Gilligein, Charles Tigny, mis- sing.

A. B. HOWARD, Ad't 9th Reg't, 3d Brigade.

[Official]

A. B. Hendren, Maj. & A. A. G. 3d Brig

While in Milledgeville, Sherman made his headquarters in the Executive mansion. Our informant saw, and was catechised by Gen. Jeff. Davis and Kilpatrick. The State House was not burned, but much mutilated. The Penitentiary, Arsenal, &c., were burned. The magazine was blown up by the rear guard as they left the city Friday 10, A. M. We heard the double report, and thought them signal guns. The bridge was also burned, but Gen. Furguson had constructed pontoons for his wagons to cross.

From the best authority, General Kilpatrick commanded the left wing of the enemy, which passed along the county line road, from Milledgeville to Shoals of Ogeechee, where they camped on Friday night. They spread out some six or eight miles on either hand, pilfering and burning as they went. Seven miles below this place a ruffian presented a pistol to the breast of a lady, demanding her gold and silver. She told him she had none, and called upon an officer in the crowd for protection. Without specially granting it, he informed her rather egotistically that he was General Kilpatrick, and permitted his men to go on and pilfer and house as much as they pleased. They burned the gin houses of a number of our largest planters, with hundreds of bales of cotton. Among them, Judge Thomas', Col. Turner's, the Sasnetts, Dr. Green's, the Dickinson's &c. They burned no cribs or dwelling houses, and we have no reliable information of the destruction of a single mill or factory in the country, though they passed by a number.— They took nearly all the horses and mules in the country, whether hid or not, for they scoured the swamps, killed some hogs and most of the poultry. The productive interest of the country has suffered seriously—irreparably, we fear. All the young negro men and some women they captured where they were not run off. Many of these have returned, and are still coming back as they can escape.

BIBLIOGRAPHY:

Battles & Leaders of The Civil War, Volume IV, Secaucus, New Jersey, 1982.

Blue & Gray Magazine, Winter 1996.

Bragg, William Harris A Little Battle At Griswoldville, Civil War Times

Bridges, Jonathan, Letters of Jonathan Bridges a Confederate Soldier of Stewart County, Georgia, R. & D. Patchin, 1985.

Bull, Rice. Soldiering. Jack Bauer, ed. San Rafael, California: Presidio Press, 1977.

Chronicle & Sentinel Newspaper, November 30, 1864.

Clark, Walter A., Under the Stars and Bars, Jonesboro, Georgia, Freedom Hill Press, 1987.

Collman, Kenneth, Confederate Athens, Athens, Georgia, University of Georgia Press, 1969.

Confederate Veteran Magazine, Volumes 1, 18, 27 & 39.

Connolly, James Austin, Three Years in the Army of the Cumberland: The Letters and Diary of Major James A. Connolly. Edited by Paul M. Angle, Bloomington, Indiana: University Press, 1959.

Daily Constitution News. Augusta: November 30, 1864.

Davidson, Victor, History off Wilkinson County, Macon, Georgia, J.W. Burke Company, 1930.

Davis, Burke. Sherman's March. New York: Random House,

1980.

Davis, Robert Scott Jr., <u>A History of Montgomery County,</u>
<u>Georgia to 1918.</u> Montgomery County, 1993.

Dozer, Jesse L., <u>Marching With Sherman Through Georgia and</u>
<u>the Carolinas, Civil War Diary of Jesse L. Dozer,</u> edited by
Wilfred W. Black, Collections of the Georgia Historical
Society.

Dyer. John P., <u>The Gallant Hood,</u> New York, Konecky &
Konecky, 1950.

Eisenschiml, Otto & Newman, Ralph, <u>The Civil War: An</u>
<u>American Iliad,</u> New York, Konecky & Konecky, 1956.

Evans, Clement A., ed. <u>Confederate Military History,</u> Volume
VIII, Atlanta: Confederate Publishing Company, 1899.

Fisher, John E., <u>They Rode with Forrest and Wheeler,</u> Jefferson,
North Carolina, McFarland & Company, Inc., 1995.

<u>Folio on Griswoldville.</u> Vol III. University of Georgia Library.
Macon.

Glatthaar, Joseph T., <u>The March to the Sea and Beyond,</u>
<u>Shermans Troops in the Savannah and Carolinas Campaigns,</u>
New York, New York University Press, 1985.

Gragg, Rod, <u>The Illustrated Confederate Reader,</u> New York,
Harper & Row, 1989.

Guernsey & Alden, <u>Harpers Pictorial History of the Civil War,</u>
New York, Fairfax Press, 1886.

<u>Georgia Historical Markers,</u> Helen, Georgia, Bay Tree Grove,
1973.

200

King, Jack N., personal papers, Macon, 1864.

King, Spencer B. , <u>Sounds of Drums</u>, Macon, Mercer University Press, 1984.

Lane, Mills, <u>Dear Mother: Don't grieve about me. If I get killed, I'll only be dead.</u>, Savannah, Beehive Press Book, 1990.

Lewis, Lloyd, <u>Sherman Fighting Prophet,</u> New York, Konecky & Konecky, 1932.

Lawliss, Chuck, <u>The Civil War Source Book,</u> New York, Random House, 1991.

Malcom, Frank, "'Such is War': The Letters of an Orderly in the 7th Iowa Infantry.", Edited by James I. Robertston, Jr. <u>Iowa Journal of History,</u> vol. 58, October 1960.

McInvale, Morton R. "'All That Devils Could Wish For". The Griswoldville Campaign, November, 1864," <u>Georgia Historical Quarterly.</u> Vol. 60, Summer, 1976.

Miles, Jim, <u>To The Sea</u>. Nashville. Rutledge Hill Press, 1989.

Nichols, George Ward. <u>The Story of the Great March.</u> New York: Harper and Brothers, 1865.

Nugent, William Lewis, <u>My Dear Nellie: The Civil War Letters of William L. Nugent to Eleanor Smith Nugent.</u> Edited by William M. Cash and Lucy Somerville Howorth, Jackson: University Press of Mississippi, 1977.

<u>Rebellion Records, 1864.</u>

Reynolds, Jno. C., <u>Dickey Letters,</u> Macon, 1864.

Scaife, William R. <u>The March to the Sea.</u> Washington Printing

Company, 1989.

Sherman, William T., Memoirs of General William T. Sherman, New York, 1875.

Sifakis, Stewart, Who Was Who in the Union, Facts on File, Inc., New York, 1988.

Stegeman, John F., These Men She Gave, Civil War Diary of Athens, Georgia, Athens, University of Georgia Press.

Southern Banner Newspaper. Athens. November 30, 1864.

Taylor, Richard, Destruction and Reconstruction, New York, D. Appleton and Company, 1879.

Upson, Theodore F. With Sherman to the Sea. Oscar Osburn Winther, ed. Baton Rouge: Louisiana State University Press, 1943.

Southern Historical Society Papers, vol. 13.

Telegraph & Confederate Newspaper. Macon. November 24, 1864 & November 30, 1864.

Wells, Charles. The Battle of Griswoldville. Macon. Wells.

Wheeler, Richard. Sherman's March. New York. Crowell Publishing. 1978.

Williams, Carolyn White. History of Jones County Georgia. Macon. The J.W. Burke Company. 1957.

Wiley, Bell Irvin, The Life of Johnny Reb, New York, Grosset & Dunlap,

War of the Rebellion. Volumes 44, 45 part I, and 53.

REFERENCE NOTES

ABBREVIATIONS

ALB - William Harris Bragg, "A Little Battle at Griswoldville," *Civil WarTimes Illustrated*, vol. (   ) pp. 44-49.

ATD - Morton R. McInvale, "All That Devils Could Wish For, The Griswoldville Campaign November 1864. *The Georgia Historical Quarterly*, vol. 60 (1976)

B & L - *Battles & Leaders of the Civil War*, 5 vols. Secaucus, 1982, vol. 4 unless otherwise stated.

CV- Confederate Veteran

DM - Lane, Mills. *Dear Mother: Don't grieve about me. If I get killed, I'll only be dead.* Savannah, 1990.

FOG - *Folio on* Griswoldville, vol. III unless otherwise stated.

LOJB - *Letters of Jonathan Bridges, A Confederate Soldier of Stewart County, Georgia.*

MTTS - William R. Scaife, *The March to the Sea*, Atlanta, 1989.

MWS - Jesse L. Dozer, *Marching with Sherman Through Georgia and the Carolinas,Civil War Diary of Jesse L. Dozer*, pt. 1, Edited by Wilfred W. Black.*Georgia Historical Quarterly*, vol. 52, (1968) pp. 454-473.

OR - U.S. War Department, *The War of the Rebellion: A Compilation of the Official Records of the Union and Confederate Armies.* 128 vols. Washington, D.C.,1890-1901. All references are to series I unless otherwise noted.

SD - Rice Bull, *Soldiering, A Civil War Diary, 123 N.Y. Vol. Infantry.* Edited by Jack Bauer, San Rafael, 1977.

SM - Burke Davis, *Sherman's March*, New York, 1980.

TBG - Charles Wells, *The Battle of Griswoldville*, Macon, 1961.

TTS - Jim Miles, *To The Sea*, Nashville, 1989.

WSS - Theodore F. Upson, *With Sherman to the Sea*, Baton Rouge, 1943.

NOTES

Chapter 1 "Hurricane Sherman"

1. Bridges Smith, *CV*, vol. 39, (1929) p. 105.
2. *B & L*, vol. IV, p. 667.
3. Ibid.
4. Robert Scott Davis, Jr., *A History of Montgomery County, Georgia to 1918*, (1993), pp. 206-207.
5. Ibid.
6. *OR* 53, pt 1, p. 44.
7. ALB, p. 45.
8. Ibid.
9. *TTS*, p. 139.
10. Kenneth Coleman, *Confederate Athens*, (Athens, 1967) p.99.
11. Ibid.
12. LOJB, Bridges to wife, November 12, 1864, near Lovejoy Station.
13. *TTS*, P. 142.
14. *CV* 27, p. 469.
15. Carolyn White Williams, *History of Jones County Georgia*, (Macon, 1957) p. 159.
16. Ibid.
17. Thomas S. Campbell Letters, microfilm reel 56, drawer 80.
18. *Confederate Military History: Extended Edition*, vol. VII-Alabama, (Wilmington, 1899) p. 876.
19. Ibid.
20. Ibid.

21. Victor Davidson, *History of Wilkinson County*, (Macon, 1930) p. 259.

Chapter 2 "Now You Must Go"

1. *TTS*, p. 5.
2. Ibid., p. 15.
3. John E. Fisher, *They Rode with Forrest and Wheeler*, (Jefferson, 1995) p. 120.
4. *OR* 39, pt. 3, p. 594.
5. Ibid.
6. Ibid., p. 679.
7. *TTS*, p. 7.
8. Ibid.9. Ibid.
10. Ibid.
11. Ibid.
12. Ibid., pp. 34-35.
13. Ibid.
14. Ibid., p. 37.
15. John P. Dyer, *The Gallant Hood*, (New York, 1950) p. 282.
16. *WSS*, p. 133.
17. Ibid.
18. Dyer, *The Gallant Hood*, pp. 21-22.
19. Jacob D. Cox, *The March to the Sea - Franklin and Nashville*, (New York, 1882) pp. 23-24.
20. Dyer, *The Gallant Hood*, pp. 21-22.
21. *TTS*, p.22.
22. George Ward Nichols, *The Story of the Great March*, (New York, 1865).
23. *MTTS*, p. 29.
24. *B & L*, vol. 4, p. 672.
25. Richard Wheeler, *Sherman's March*, (New

York, 1978) p. 60.

26. *TTS*, p. 29.

27. Lloyd Lewis, *Sherman Fighting Prophet*, (New York, 1932) p. 436.

28. Ibid.

29. *MTTS*, p. 24.

30. Wheeler, *Sherman's March*, p.61.

31. *WSS*, p. 133.

32. *Telegraph & Confederate*, Macon newspaper, November 25, 1864.

33. *TTS*, p. 26.

34. Ibid.

35. Ibid.

36. Ibid.

37. Ibid., p. 27.

38. Guernsey & Alden, *Harpers Pictorial History of the Civil* War, (New York, 1866) p. 685.

39. Ibid., pp. 685-686.

40. Ibid., p. 686.

41. *FOG*, p. 103.

42. Ibid.

43. *MWS*, p. 454.

44. Ibid.

45. *MTTS*, p. 29.

46. *WSS*, p. 134.

47. James Auston Connolly, *Three Years in the Army of the Cumberland: The Letters and Diary of Major James A. Connolly.* (Bloomington, 1959), p. 301.

48. Frank Malcom, "Such is War": The Letters of an Orderly in the 7th Iowa Infantry, *Iowa Journal of History,* vol. 58, (October 1960) p. 340.

Chapter 3 "Joe Wheeler: The War Child"

1. *TTS*, p. 105.
2. Ibid.
3. ALB, p. 45.
4. Bell Irvin Wiley, *The Life of Johnny Reb*, (New York, 1971) pp. 342-343.
5. *B & L*, p. 332.
6. Ibid.
7. Sam R. Watkins, *"Co AYTCH"A Side Show of the Big Show*, (Wilmington, 1994) pp. 189-190.
8. Ibid.
9. John F. Stegeman, *These Men She Gave, Civil War Diary of Athens, Georgia*, (Athens) p. 133.
10. Guernsey & Alden, *Harpers Pictorial History of the Civil War*, pp. 613-614.
11. ALB, p. 45.
12. *B & L*, vol. 4, p. 667.
13. Fisher, *They Rode with Forrest and Wheeler*, p. 120.
14. *TTS*, p. 140.
15. Ibid.
16. Ibid.
17. Ibid., p. 141.
18. Ibid., p. 140.
19. *CV* 38, p. 78.
20. *Confederate Military History*, vol. 8, p. 372.
21. William Lewis Nugent, *My Dear Nellie: The Civil War Letters of William L. Nugent to Eleanor Smith Nugent.* (Jackson) p. 129.

Chapter 4 "Skirmish at Lovejoy Station"

1. *TTS*, p. 142.
2. *Confederate Military History,* vol. 8, p. 372.
3. *MTTS*, p. 31.
4. *TTS*, p. 142.
5. *Telegraph & Confederate*, Macon newspaper, November 24, 1864.
6. *TTS*, p. 142.
7. Davis, *History of Montgomery County,* pp. 206-207.
8. ATD, p. 117.
9. *Confederate Military History,* vol. 8, p. 372.

Chapter 5 "Let All of Her Sons Come to Her rescue"

1. *OR* 45, pt. 1, p. 1214.
2. Ibid.
3. Ibid., p. 1215.
4. Ibid.
5. Ibid.
6. Ibid., p. 1216.
7. Ibid., p. 1217.
8. Ibid., pp. 1217-1218.
9. *TTS*, p. 143.
10. Ibid.
11. Ibid.
12. *OR* 45, pt. 1, p. 1225.
13. William T. Sherman, *Memoirs of General T. Sherman,* (New York, 1875) p. 665.
14. *FOG*, pp. 86-87.
15. Walter Clark, *Under the Stars and Bars,* (Jonesboro, 1987) pp. 167-168.
16. Spencer B. King, *Sound of Drums,* (Macon, 1984) p. 253.

17. *OR* 45, pt. 1, p. 1236.

Chapter 6 "Ceaseless War. God Help Us"

1. *TTS*, p. 142.
2. Ibid.
3. *Confederate Military History*, vol. 8, p. 372.
4. *DM*, p. XXVII
5. LOJB.
6. *TTS*, p. 142.
7. Ibid.
8. *Confederate Military History*, vol. 8, p. 372.
9. *TTS*, p. 142.
10. Ibid., p. 143.
11. King, *Sounds of* Drums, pp. 152-154.
12. Ibid.
13. Ibid.
14. *TTS*, p. 153.
15. Ibid.
16. Ibid.
17. *Rebellion Records 1864*, pp. 158-159.
18. Joseph Glathaar, *The March to the Sea and Beyond*, (New York, 1985) p. 160.
19. *B & L*, p. 667.
20. Ibid.
21. Davis, *History of Montgomery County*, pp. 206-207.
22. *DM*, pp. 335-336.
23. *B & L*, p. 667.
24. *DM*, pp. 334-335.
25. ATD, pp. 118-119.
26. *MTTS*, pp. 32-33.
27. Ibid., pp. iii - iv.

28. Ibid.
29. Ibid.
30. *DM,*pp. 334-335.
31. Davis, *The History of Montgomery County,* pp. 206 - 207.
32. ATD, pp. 118 - 119.
33. *MWS,* pt. 1, p. 454.
34. *MTTS,* p. 28.
35. ATD, pp. 118 - 119.
36. *B & L,* p. 667.
37. Ibid., p. 332.
38. Ibid., p. 667.
39. Ibid., p. 142.
40. *Confederate Military History,* vol. 8, p. 378.
41. *TTS,* p. 50.
42. Ibid., p. 51.
43. *MWS,* p. 455.
44. *WSS,* pp. 135-136.
45. Ibid.
46. Ibid.
47. King, *Sounds of Drums,* p. 147.
48. ATD, p. 120.
49. King, *Sounds of Drums,* p.22.
50. *TBG,* p. 3.
51. Ibid.
52. *CV* 1, p. 147.
53. King, *Sounds of Drums,* p. 441.
54. *TTS,* pp. 53-54.
55. Ibid.
56. Ibid.
57. Ibid.
58. King, *Sound of Drums,* pp. 447 - 448.
59. Rod Gragg, *The Illustrated Confederate*

Reader, (New York, 1989) pp. 175 - 176.
60. King, *Sound of Drums,* p. 448.
61. Ibid., p. 450.
62. Ibid.
63. *MWS,* p. 455.
64. *OR* 53, p. 27.
65. *TTS,* p. 65.
66. *B & L,* p. 667.
67. *DM,* pp. 334-335.
68. *TTS,* p. 144.
69. *OR* 53, p. 32.
70. *TTS,* p. 155.
71. Ibid., p. 57.
72. *SD,* p. 186.
73. *TTS,* pp. 143 - 144.
74. *Rebellion Records 1864,* p. 162.
75. Ibid.
76. Ibid., pp. 162 - 163.
77. *TTS,* pp. 144 - 145.
78. *B & L,* p. 667.
79. *TTS,* pp. 144- 145.
80. Ibid.
81. *Chronicle & Sentinel,* newspaper, November 30, 1864.
82. *DM,* pp. 334-336.
83. *Chronicle & Sentinel,* newspaper, November 30, 1864.
84. *B & L,* p. 667.
85. King, *Sound of Drums,* pp. 185 - 187.
86. Chuck Lawliss, *The Civil War Source Book,* (New York, 1991) p. 164.
87. Ibid.
88. ATD, p. 120.
89. *MWS,* p. 455.
90. *FOG,* p. 66.

Chapter 7 Thin Gray Line

1. ATD, p. 122.
2. *FOG* p. 88.
3. *MWS*, p. 455.
4. *TTS*, p. 65.
5. *Rebellion Records 1864*, pp. 162 - 163.
6. *TBG*, pp. 2 - 4.
7. Ibid.
8. Ibid.
9. King, *Sound of Drums*, pp. 260 - 261.
10. Augustus Pitts Adamson, *Brief History of Thirtieth Georgia Regiment*, (1962)
11. *Rebellion Records 1864*, pp. 162 - 163.
12. Ibid., p. 171.
13. Ibid., pp. 162 - 163, 171.
14. Ibid., p. 171.
15. *SD*, p. 186.
16. *FOG*, p. 75.
17. ALB, p. 45.
18. *TTS,* p. 65.
19. *MTTS,* pp. 32 - 33.
20. *Rebellion Records 1864*, p. 159.
21. Ibid.
22. *Telegraph & Confederate* newspaper, November 25, 1864.
23. *Rebellion Records 1864*, p. 159.
24. *TTS*, p. 140.
25. Ibid.
26. *MTTS*, p. 36.
27. *B & L*, p. 667.
28. Ibid.
29. *MTTS*, pp. 41 - 42.

30. *WSS*, pp. 137 - 138.
31. *Rebellion Records 1864*, p. 170.
32. *TTS*, p. 65.
33. *OR* 39, pt. 1, p. 101.
34. Williams, *History of Jones County*, pp. 159 - 160.
35. *TTS*, p. 65.
36. ALB, p. 45.

37. *Georgia Historic Markers*, (Helen, 1973) p. 318.

Chapter 8 "Let All of Them Get Warm By The Fire"

1. *SM*, pp. 51 - 52.
2. Richard Taylor, *Destruction and Reconstruction*, (New York, 1879) pp. 210 211.
3. Ibid.
4. Ibid.
5. Ibid.
6. Ibid.
7. Ibid.
8. Ibid.
9. Ibid.
10. Ibid., p. 53.
11. *FOG*, p. 66.
12. ALB, p. 45.
13. *B & L*, p. 667.
14. Ibid.
15. Taylor, *Destruction and Reconstruction*, p. 112.
16. Ibid.

Chapter 9   "Avoid a Fight With a Superior Force"

1. *Confederate Military History,* p. 372.
2. *SD,* p. 186.
3. *MTTS,* p. 29.
4. *Rebellion Records 1864,* p. 163.
5. *MWS,* p. 455.
6. *OR* 39, pt. 1, p. 97.
7. Ibid.
8. *Rebellion Records 1864,* p. 159.
9. Ibid.
10. Ibid.
11. Ibid.
12. Ibid.
13. ATD, p. 123.
14. *TTS,* p. 145.
15. *OR* 53, p. 41.
16. *TTS,* p. 146.
17. *OR* 53, p. 41.
18. *OR* 39, pt. 1, p. 101.
19. Ibid.
20. *TBG,* p. 6.
21. *OR* 39, pt. 1, p. 101.
22. *Rebellion Records 1864,* p. 159.
23. Ibid.
24. Ibid.
25. *OR* 39, pt. 1, p. 105.
26. Ibid.
27. Ibid.
28. *CV,* vol. 27, p. 469.
29. *OR* 53, p. 41.
30. *DM,* pp. 335-336.
31. *OR* 53, p. 41.

32. Ibid.
33. Ibid., p. 42.
34. Davis, *History of Montgomery County*, pp. 206 - 207.
35. *OR* 53, p. 39.
36. Ibid.
37. Ibid.
38. Ibid.
39. Ibid., p. 41.
40. Ibid.
41. *FOG*, p. 105.
42. *OR* 53, p. 41.
43. Ibid.
44. Ibid.

Chapter 10   "Not Dreaming of a Fight"

1. *OR* 53, pp. 27 - 28.
2. Ibid.
3. ALB, p. 47.
4. *TBG*, p. 11.
5. ALB, p. 47.
6. *OR* 39, pt. 1, p. 108.
7. *OR* 53, p. 28.
8. Ibid., p. 41.
9. Eisenschiml & Newman, *The Civil War: An American Iliad,* (New York, 1956) p. 654.
10. ALB, p. 47.
11. *OR* 53, p. 28.
12. Ibid., p. 29.
13. *OR* 39, pt. 1, p. 107.
14. Ibid., p. 105.
15. ALB, p. 47.

16. Ibid., p. 48.
17. *OR* 53, p. 41.
18. *SM*, p. 55.
19. ALB, p. 47.
20. *MTTS*, p. 37.
21. Eisenschiml & Newman, *The Civil War: An American Iliad*, p. 654.
22. *FOG*, p. 76.
23. *OR* 53, p. 41.
24. ATD, p. 125.
25. *OR* 53, p. 41.
26. *DM*, pp. 334 - 336.
27. ATD, p. 125.
28. *OR* 53, p. 41.
29. Ibid., p. 31.
30. Ibid., p. 39.
31. ALB, p. 47.
32. *OR* 53, p. 40.
33. Ibid.
34. *SD*, p. 186.

Chapter 11 "It Was a Terrible Sight"

1. King, *Sound of Drums*, p. 380.
2. Victor Davidson, *History of Wilkinson County*, (Macon, 1930) p. 258.
3. Williams, *History of Jones County*, p. 158.
4. Davis, *History of Montgomery County*, pp. 206 - 207.
5. Ibid.
6. *FOG*, p. 66.
7. Davidson, *History of Wilkinson County*, p. 259.
8. *OR* 53, p. 43.

9. Ibid.

10. Ibid.

11. Ibid.

12. Eisenschiml & Newman, *The Civil War: An American Iliad,* p. 654.

13. *OR* 53, p. 28.

14. Ibid.

15. *TBG*, p. 11.

16. *OR* 39, pt. 1, p. 105.

17. Eisenschiml & Newman, *The Civil War: An American Iliad,* p. 654

18. *FOG*, p. 66.

19. *SM*, p. 55.

20. Wheeler, *Sherman's March,* p. 64.

21. *FOG*, p. 76.

22. Ibid., p. 66.

23. ALB, p. 47.

24. Ibid., p. 48.

25. *OR* 39, pt. 1, p. 105.

26. ALB, p. 48.

27. Eisenschiml & Newman, *The Civil War: An American Iliad,* p. 654.

28. David, *History of Montgomery County,* pp. 206-207.

29. *OR* 39, pt. 1, p. 105.

30. Williams, *History of Jones County,* p. 259.

31. *OR* 53, p. 29.

32. *WSS*, pp. 136 - 137.

33. *SM*, p.55.

34. *TBG*, p. 11.

35. *OR* 53, pp. 43 - 44.

36. Ibid.

37. *MTTS*, map of Griswoldville battle.

38. ALB, p. 48.
39. *OR* 53, p. 42.
40. Ibid.
41. Ibid.
42. Ibid., p. 44.
43. Ibid.
44. Ibid.
45. Ibid.
46. *OR* 39, pt. 1, p. 108.
47. Ibid., p. 28.
48. Ibid.
49. *OR* 39, pt. 1, p. 105.
50. Ibid.
51. *TTS*, p. 158.
52. *OR* 39, pt. 1, p. 105.
53. Ibid., p. 107.
54. *SM*, pp. 55 -56.
55. *OR* 39, pt. 1, p. 107.
56. Williams, *History of Jones County*, p. 159.
57. *FOG*, p. 76.
58. *OR* 53, p. 44.
59. *Southern Banner*, Athens newspaper,
    November 30, 1864.
60. *DM*, pp. 335-336.
61. *FOG*, p. 91.
62. *WSS*, p. 137.
63. *OR* 53, p. 29.
64. *SM*, p. 55.
65. *WSS*, p. 137.
66. *OR* 53, p. 28.
67. *TTS*, p. 147.
68. *Daily Constitutional News*, Augusta newspaper,
    November 30, 1864.

69. Ibid.
70. Ibid.
71. Ibid.
72. Ibid.
73. Ibid.
74. *Southern Banner,* Athens newspaper, November 30, 1864.
75. *OR* 53, p. 28.
76. Ibid., p. 42.
77. Ibid., p. 44.
78. Ibid., p. 40.
79. ALB, p. 48.
80. Ibid., p. 44.
81. Ibid., p. 43.
82. *OR* 53, p. 28.
83. *OR* 39, pt. 1, p. 108.
84. *Telegraph & Confederate,* Macon newspaper, November 24, 1864.
85. Ibid.
86. Davis, *History of Montgomery County,* pp. 206-207.
87. *Telegraph & Confederate,* Macon newspaper, November 24, 1864.
88. *OR* 53, p. 28.
89. Ibid., p. 43.
90. Ibid., p. 42.
91. Ibid.
92. *Chronicle & Sentinel*, newspaper, November 30, 1864.
93. *OR* 53, p. 28.
94. *Telegraph & Confederate,* Macon newspaper, November 24, 1864.
95. King, *Sound of Drums,* p. 157.

96. ALB, p. 49.
97. *OR* 39, pt. 1, p. 102.
98. *Rebellion Records 1864*, p. 159.
99. *OR* 53, p. 44.
100. Ibid., p. 42.
101. Ibid., p. 43.
102. Davis, *History of Montgomery County*, pp. 206 - 207.
103. ALB, p. 49.
104. *OR* 53, p. 42.
105. *OR* 39, pt. 1, p. 105.
106. Ibid.
107. *SM*, p. 56.
108. *WSS*, p. 138.
109. Ibid.
110. *SM*, p. 56.
111. *TTS*, p. 148.
112. ATD, p. 128.
113. Glathaar, *The March to Sea and Beyond*, p. 161.
114. *Telegraph & Confederate*, Macon newspaper, November 30, 1864.

Chapter 12 "Among Them are Some of My Best Men and Officers"

1. *SD*, p. 187.
2. Williams, *History of Jones County*, p. 160.
3. *Chronicle & Sentinel*, newspaper, November 30, 1864.
4. *WSS*, p. 138.
5. *OR* 53, p. 28.
6. *OR* 39, pt. 1, p. 107.

7. Ibid., p. 108.
8. Ibid., p. 98.
9. Ibid., pp. 105 - 106.
10. Ibid.
11. *FOG*, p. 74.
12. ALB, p. 49.
13. *FOG*, p.74.
14. *WSS*, p. 137.
15. *MWS*, p. 455.
16. ALB, p. 49.
17. LOJB, p. 58.
18. Ibid.
19. *OR* 53, pp. 40 - 41.
20. Williams, *History of Jones County*, p. 259.
21. *Southern Banner*, Athens newspaper, November 30, 1864.
22. Davis, *History of Montgomery County*, pp. 206 - 207.
23. LOJB, p. 58.
24. *CV*, vol. 39, p. 105.
25. *DM*, pp. 335-336.
26. ALB, p. 49.
27. Civil war Miscillary, Personal Papers of Jack N. King, Georgia Militia, folder, King to Wife, November 23, 1864, from Macon Georgia.
28. Davis, *History of Montgomery County*, pp. 206 - 207.
29. *DM*, pp. 335-336.
30. *FOG*, p. 74.
31. Fisher, *They Rode With Forrest*, p. 121.
32. Taylor, *Destruction & Reconstruction*, p. 212.
33. *OR* 53, p. 42.
34. Ibid., p. 43.

35. Ibid., p. 44.
36. *B & L,* vol. IV, p. 667.
37. ALB, p. 49.
38. Ibid.
39. Dickey Letters series, Drawer 49, Microfilm Roll 78.
40. *OR* 39, pt. 1, p. 106.
41. Ibid., p. 98.
42. Ibid., p. 99.
43. *TTS,* p. 158.
44. *SD,* p. 187.
45. Williams, *History of Jones County,* p. 160.
46. King, *Sound of Drums,* pp. 155 - 157.
47. *FOG,* p. 177.
48. *Southern Banner,* Athens newspaper, November 30, 1864.
49. *Telegraph & Confederate,* Macon newspaper, November 23, 1864.
50. Ibid., November 24, 1864.
51. Ibid.
52. King, *Sound of Drums,* p. 381.
53. *TTS,* p. 154.
54. LOJB, p. 58 - 59.
55. *OR* 45, p. 650.
56. King, *Sound of Drums,* p. 60.

Chapter 13 Epilogue

1. *Southern Historical Society Papers,* vol. 13, p. 360.
2. Stewart Sifakis, *Who Was Who in the Union,* vol. 1, (New York, 1989) p. 70.
3. *WSS,* p. 138.

4. *MWS*, p. 473.
5. *Confederate Military History*, p. 372.
6. *CV*, vol. 27, p. 469.
7. Ibid., vol. 39, p. 105.
8. *FOG*, p. 91.
9. Stegman, *These Men She Gave*, (Athens) p. 133.
10. *TBG*, p. 6.
11. Ibid.
12. Griswoldville Battle Site Acquired, *Blue and Gray Magazine*, Winter 1996, p. 37.
13. *Daily Constitutional*, Augusta newspaper, November 30, 1864.
14. *Southern Historical Society Papers*, vol. 13, pp. 366 - 367.
15. Ibid.
16. *OR* 53, p. 38.
17. Williams, *History of Jones County*, p. 259.
18. King, *Sound of Drums*, p. 154.
19. *TBG*, p. 11.